GOODSON MUMBA

THE WEALTH OF NATIONS REIMAGINED

Understanding Economics in the Modern World

Copyright © 2024 by Goodson Mumba

All rights reserved. No part of this publication may be reproduced, stored or transmitted in any form or by any means, electronic, mechanical, photocopying, recording, scanning, or otherwise without written permission from the publisher. It is illegal to copy this book, post it to a website, or distribute it by any other means without permission.

First edition

ISBN: 9798334768819

This book was professionally typeset on Reedsy. Find out more at reedsy.com

Contents

Preface		iv
Acknowledgement		vii
Dedication		viii
Disclaimer		ix
1	Chapter 1: Foundation of Modern Economics	1
2	Chapter 2: Markets and Competition	14
3	Chapter 3: Labor and Human Capital	33
4	Chapter 4: Money, Banking, and Monetary Policy	49
5	Chapter 5: Economic Growth and Development	66
6	Chapter 6: International Trade and Finance	84
7	Chapter 7: Public Finance and Fiscal Policy	103
8	Chapter 8: Behavioral Economics	122
9	Chapter 9: Innovation and Technological Change	141
10	Chapter 10: Environmental Economics	161
11	Chapter 11: Urban and Regional Economics	181
12	Chapter 12: Health Economics	200
13	Chapter 13: Economic Policy Analysis	219
14	Chapter 14: Emerging Trends in Economics	237
15	Chapter 15: Economics and Society	256
About the Author		277

Preface

The profound impact of economics on our daily lives is undeniable, yet its complexities often remain shrouded in mystery for many. In an era of rapid technological advancements, global interconnectivity, and unprecedented challenges, understanding the principles that govern our economic systems is more crucial than ever. "The Wealth of Nations Reimagined: Understanding Economics in the Modern World" seeks to unravel these complexities and offer a comprehensive exploration of contemporary economic thought and practice.

Our journey takes us through the evolution of economic theories, the dynamics of modern markets, the intricacies of fiscal and monetary policies, and the critical role of innovation and technological change.

The setting for our exploration is Ndola, a city rich in history and cultural diversity, embodying the challenges and opportunities that define the modern economic landscape. Through the eyes of Kato, our guide and protagonist, we delve into the lived experiences of individuals and communities as they navigate the complexities of economic realities. Kato's narrative provides a human touch to the theoretical concepts, making them accessible and relatable.

"The Wealth of Nations Reimagined" is structured to provide a holistic understanding of economics. Each chapter addresses a core aspect of economic theory and practice, broken down into subpoints that explore specific topics in depth. From the historical context of economic thought to the transformative potential of economics as a tool for social change, this book covers a wide array of subjects designed to inform, challenge, and inspire.

Our approach is interdisciplinary, recognizing that economics does not operate in a vacuum. We consider the intersections with sociology, politics, environmental science, and technology, acknowledging that these fields collectively shape our economic realities. By doing so, we aim to provide a richer, more nuanced understanding of how economics influences and is influenced by the world around us.

This book is intended for a diverse audience. Whether you are a student beginning your journey into economic studies, a professional seeking to enhance your understanding of modern economic issues, or a curious reader eager to comprehend the forces shaping our world, "The Wealth of Nations Reimagined" offers valuable insights and practical knowledge.

In writing this book, we are guided by the belief that a well-informed society is better equipped to address the economic challenges and opportunities of our time. We hope to empower readers with the knowledge needed to engage thoughtfully in economic discourse and to contribute meaningfully to the development of equitable and sustainable economic policies.

We invite you to embark on this journey with us, to explore the rich tapestry of economic thought, and to envision a future where the principles of economics serve to enhance the wellbeing of all.

Welcome to "The Wealth of Nations Reimagined: Understanding Economics in the Modern World."
Goodson Mumba

Acknowledgement

I would like to eternally and gratefully acknowledge the Almighty God for the infinite intelligence from His universal mind where we draw from all that we come to know and are yet to know. May I also acknowledge and thank everyone that has played a part in my journey of life in terms of spiritual, moral, emotional and material support.

Dedication

I extend my sincerest gratitude to my beloved wife, Edith Mumba, and our children, Angelina, Lubuto, Letticia, Lulumbi, and Butusho, for their unwavering support and understanding throughout the conception, writing, and eventual publication of this book, despite the sacrifices and challenges they endured.

Disclaimer

This book is a work of fiction. Names, characters, businesses, places, events, and incidents are either the products of the author's imagination or used in a fictitious manner. Any resemblance to actual persons, living or dead, or actual events is purely coincidental.

1

Chapter 1: Foundation of Modern Economics

The Historical Context of Economic Thought

"Seeds of Change: The Economic Awakening of Ndola"

In the heart of Ndola, Zambia, Kato sits under the shade of a baobab tree, flipping through the pages of "The Wealth of Nations Reimagined." As he reads about the historical context of economic thought, his mind drifts to the story of his ancestors, who toiled the land for generations, their dreams stifled by poverty and limited opportunities.

Kato's thoughts wander back to a time when Ndola was a bustling trading post, a beacon of commerce in the region. He recalls tales of prosperity and abundance, passed down through generations, when merchants from distant lands traversed the ancient trade routes, exchanging goods and ideas with the locals.

But as colonial powers carved up Africa, Ndola's fortunes

began to wane. The once-thriving markets fell silent, replaced by foreign-owned plantations and mines that exploited the land and its people for profit. Kato's ancestors struggled to make ends meet, their labor enriching others while their own aspirations remained unfulfilled.

Driven by a desire to understand his heritage and reclaim his community's economic sovereignty, Kato immerses himself in the teachings of economic pioneers like Adam Smith. He learns how their ideas challenged the prevailing notions of mercantilism and feudalism, advocating for free markets, individual liberty, and the pursuit of self-interest.

Inspired by the resilience of those who came before him, Kato begins to see parallels between the struggles of the past and the challenges facing Ndola today. He realizes that to chart a new course for his community, he must first understand the forces that shaped its economic destiny.

As Kato continues to delve into the pages of "The Wealth of Nations Reimagined," he feels a sense of empowerment wash over him. He sees himself not just as a passive observer of history, but as an active participant in the ongoing saga of economic transformation.

With newfound clarity and purpose, Kato sets out to honor the legacy of his ancestors by rekindling the spirit of enterprise in Ndola. Armed with the wisdom of the past and the vision of the future, he embarks on a journey to sow the seeds of change and cultivate a brighter tomorrow for generations to come.

The Economic Thinkers and Their Contributions

"Echoes of Wisdom: Unveiling the Economic Thinkers of Ndola"

As Kato delves deeper into "The Wealth of Nations Reimagined," he becomes captivated by the stories of the economic thinkers who dared to challenge conventional wisdom and reshape the world around them. Inspired by their courage and innovation, Kato finds himself drawn to the task of uncovering Ndola's own intellectual heritage and fostering a new generation of economic visionaries.

With a renewed sense of purpose, Kato embarks on a quest to unearth the hidden treasures of Ndola's intellectual landscape. He seeks out elders and scholars, eager to learn from their wisdom and experience. Through their tales and teachings, he discovers a rich tapestry of indigenous knowledge, passed down through generations, that speaks to the resilience and ingenuity of his people.

Among the luminaries of Ndola's intellectual tradition, Kato finds inspiration in the stories of trailblazers like Mwana Nkosi, a visionary economist who championed the principles of self-reliance and community empowerment. He learns how Mwana Nkosi challenged the status quo and advocated for indigenous economic models that prioritized local ownership and sustainable development.

As Kato immerses himself in Ndola's intellectual heritage, he uncovers a wealth of ideas and insights that resonate deeply with his own aspirations for economic renewal. He marvels at the ingenuity of thinkers who, long before the advent of modern economics, understood the importance of harnessing local resources and fostering social cohesion.

With each revelation, Kato's determination to transform

Ndola's economic landscape grows stronger. He envisions a future where the principles of equity, solidarity, and ecological stewardship guide every facet of economic life. And he is resolved to honor the legacy of Ndola's economic thinkers by carrying their torch forward into a new era of prosperity and abundance.

Armed with the wisdom of the past and the insights of the present, Kato sets out to build bridges between Ndola's rich intellectual heritage and the cutting-edge ideas of the global economic community. He envisions a world where the voices of the marginalized are heard, where economic opportunity is accessible to all, and where the spirit of innovation thrives in every corner of society.

As Kato continues his journey of discovery, he is filled with a sense of purpose and possibility. For in the stories of Ndola's economic thinkers, he sees not just a legacy to be preserved, but a beacon of hope illuminating the path toward a brighter, more prosperous future for his community and beyond.

The Evolution of Economic Systems

"Winds of Change: The Evolution of Economic Systems in Ndola"

Kato stands on the balcony of his modest home, overlooking the bustling streets of Ndola. The city hums with activity, a testament to its resilient spirit. As he delves into the next chapter of "The Wealth of Nations Reimagined," Kato begins to reflect on the evolution of economic systems that have shaped Ndola's past and present.

Kato's thoughts travel back to a time when Ndola's economy

CHAPTER 1: FOUNDATION OF MODERN ECONOMICS

was rooted in communal traditions. He recalls stories from his grandmother about how, long before colonialism, the local people thrived through cooperative farming and bartering systems. These early economic structures were built on mutual aid and shared resources, fostering a sense of unity and collective well-being.

As Kato continues to read, he learns about the disruptive impact of colonialism on these indigenous systems. The introduction of cash crops and the imposition of European trade practices transformed Ndola's economy, shifting it towards a more extractive and exploitative model. The once self-sufficient communities found themselves entangled in global markets, their livelihoods dictated by the demands of distant powers.

Yet, Kato also discovers how Ndola's people adapted and resisted. During the struggle for independence, local leaders and thinkers sought to reclaim economic control and envision a post-colonial future. They drew on a blend of traditional practices and modern economic theories, striving to create a hybrid system that could foster both growth and equity.

Inspired by this history, Kato begins to see the current economic challenges in Ndola through a new lens. He recognizes that the city's informal markets, entrepreneurial spirit, and community networks are modern echoes of the cooperative practices of the past. These elements, if harnessed effectively, could be the key to revitalizing Ndola's economy.

Determined to act, Kato organizes a series of community workshops. He brings together local business owners, farmers, and young entrepreneurs to discuss the evolution of economic systems and explore how Ndola can forge its own path forward. They talk about the importance of balancing traditional values with innovative approaches, creating an economy that is both resilient and inclusive.

Through these dialogues, Kato and his community start to develop a vision for Ndola's economic future. They imagine a city where sustainable agriculture thrives alongside tech startups, where local crafts are valued as much as global exports, and where every resident has a stake in the community's prosperity.

As Kato looks out over Ndola, he feels a renewed sense of hope. The winds of change are blowing through the city, carrying with them the promise of a brighter, more equitable future. By understanding and honoring the evolution of economic systems, Kato believes they can build an economy that reflects the best of their past and the potential of their future.

Principles of Microeconomics

"Microcosm of Change: Unveiling the Principles of Microeconomics in Ndola"

Kato sits at a small, worn desk in his community center, surrounded by eager faces. He has organized a series of evening classes to share the knowledge he's gleaned from "The Wealth of Nations Reimagined." Tonight's lesson focuses on the principles of microeconomics, a topic Kato believes is crucial for empowering his fellow residents to make informed decisions in their daily lives.

"Let's start with something simple," Kato says, holding up a loaf of bread. "How much would you pay for this?"

Hands shoot up, each person offering different amounts.

CHAPTER 1: FOUNDATION OF MODERN ECONOMICS

Kato smiles. "Exactly. The price you're willing to pay is influenced by supply and demand—one of the key principles of microeconomics."

He explains how supply and demand determine prices in the market, using examples familiar to his audience. "Think of the tomatoes sold at our local market. During the rainy season, when everyone has a bountiful harvest, the supply is high, and prices drop. But during the dry season, when fewer tomatoes are available, prices rise."

As the lesson continues, Kato delves into the concept of elasticity. "Imagine our favorite nshima seller doubles her prices overnight. How would we react?"

"We'd buy from someone else!" shouts a young man from the back, prompting laughter.

"Exactly," Kato nods. "That's elasticity—how sensitive we are to price changes. For essential goods like nshima, demand is inelastic. We need it, so we'll pay more. But for luxuries, like those imported chocolates, demand is elastic. We can easily switch to something else if the price goes up."

Kato moves on to the idea of marginal utility, picking up a mango from the desk. "The first mango you eat is delicious and satisfying. But by the third or fourth, you're less excited, right? That's diminishing marginal utility. Each additional mango gives you less satisfaction."

He illustrates the principle of opportunity cost with a local example. "Imagine you have to choose between working at the market or helping your family on the farm. If you choose the market, the opportunity cost is the time you could have spent farming. Understanding this helps us make better decisions about how to use our limited resources."

Finally, Kato discusses the importance of competition and

market structures. "In Ndola, we have many small shops selling similar goods. This competition helps keep prices fair and quality high. But what if there was only one shop? Without competition, they could charge high prices and offer poor service."

As the session ends, Kato sees the spark of understanding in his neighbors' eyes. They begin discussing how they can apply these principles to their own small businesses and daily lives, from negotiating better prices to making more informed choices about where to invest their time and money.

Kato feels a deep sense of satisfaction. By breaking down the principles of microeconomics into relatable examples, he's helping his community grasp concepts that can empower them to take control of their economic futures. He knows that this knowledge, combined with the resilience and ingenuity of Ndola's people, will be a powerful force for change.

Walking home, Kato is filled with hope. He envisions a future where the principles of microeconomics are not just abstract theories but practical tools that enable the people of Ndola to build a thriving, equitable economy from the ground up.

Principles of Macroeconomics

"Broad Horizons: Exploring the Principles of Macroeconomics in Ndola"

The community center in Ndola buzzes with anticipation as residents gather for another evening class led by Kato. Tonight, the room is filled with an even larger crowd, drawn by the promise of understanding how broader economic forces shape their daily lives. Kato stands at the front, ready to dive into the principles of macroeconomics, hoping to illuminate the bigger picture of the economy in which they all play a part.

"Good evening, everyone," Kato begins, his voice steady with enthusiasm. "Last time, we talked about the small, individual parts of our economy. Tonight, we're looking at the big picture—macroeconomics."

He starts with a simple analogy. "Imagine our community is like a big pot of stew. Each ingredient—us, our businesses, our government—contributes to the flavor. Macroeconomics is about understanding how the whole stew is cooking."

Kato introduces the concept of Gross Domestic Product (GDP). "GDP measures the total value of everything we produce in Ndola. It's like the sum of all our efforts. When our GDP grows, it means our economy is getting stronger, and we're producing more."

He explains further using Ndola's local economy. "Think about the new factories opening up, the new roads being built, or even the increased agricultural output. All these activities contribute to our GDP."

Next, Kato tackles inflation. "Have you noticed how the price of maize has gone up over the years?" Heads nod in agreement. "That's inflation—the general rise in prices. It's not just about one item getting expensive but about everything costing more over time."

To explain unemployment, Kato recounts a personal story. "My cousin, Juma, lost his job when the textile factory closed. He's one of many who are unemployed. High unemployment means our resources—our people—aren't being used effectively, and that weakens our economy."

He then addresses fiscal policy. "This is how our government spends money and collects taxes. For example, when the government builds a new school, they're spending money to create jobs and improve education. Raising taxes, on the other hand, can slow down spending but might be necessary to pay for important services."

Kato discusses monetary policy with a practical example. "When you go to the bank for a loan, the interest rate they offer you is influenced by our central bank. Lower interest rates can encourage us to borrow and spend more, boosting the economy. But if the rates are too high, we save instead of spending, which can slow the economy down."

Finally, he talks about trade balances. "Look at our exports—copper, crops, and crafts. When we export more than we import, we have a trade surplus, which is good for our economy. But if we import more than we export, we have a trade deficit, which can lead to debt."

As Kato finishes, he sees the light of understanding in the eyes of his neighbors. They start discussing how these broader forces impact their own lives and businesses, from the prices they pay at the market to the availability of jobs in Ndola.

One woman raises her hand. "Kato, how can we use this knowledge to improve our community?"

Kato smiles. "By understanding these principles, we can make better decisions and advocate for policies that support growth and stability. We can push for investment in local businesses, better education, and infrastructure. Together, we can influence how our 'stew' is cooked, ensuring it benefits everyone."

As the session ends, Kato feels a profound sense of achievement. He has opened a window into the world of macroeconomics, empowering his community to see beyond the immediate and understand the broader forces at play. Walking home, he envisions a future where Ndola's residents are not only participants in the economy but also informed architects of their own economic destiny.

The Role of Government in Economic Affairs

"Guiding Hands: The Role of Government in Economic Affairs in Ndola"

Kato stands at the front of the community center once more, ready to tackle the final subpoint of his introductory chapter. Tonight, the topic is especially relevant to the residents of Ndola: the role of government in economic affairs. The room is packed, with people eager to understand how their local and national governments influence the economy they live and work in.

"Good evening, everyone," Kato begins, his voice filled with conviction. "We've learned about the pieces of our economy and the bigger picture. Now, let's talk about the government's role in shaping our economic landscape."

He starts with a relatable example. "Think about our roads and schools. Who builds and maintains them? The government. They provide public goods—things that benefit all of us but wouldn't be profitable for private businesses to handle."

Kato explains how the government can influence economic growth through infrastructure investment. "When the government builds a new road, it's not just about making travel easier. It connects farmers to markets, helps businesses move their goods, and creates jobs. This kind of investment is crucial for our community's growth."

Next, he addresses regulation. "Do you remember the contaminated water scare last year?" The room murmurs in agreement. "The government sets regulations to ensure our water is safe, our food is healthy, and our working conditions are fair. These regulations protect us, even if they sometimes make business operations more complex."

He moves on to taxation and public spending. "Taxes might seem like a burden, but they're how the government funds essential services—like healthcare, education, and public safety. Imagine if our clinic didn't have enough doctors or our schools lacked teachers. Taxes help prevent that."

Kato discusses the role of government in stabilizing the economy. "During tough times, like droughts or economic downturns, the government can step in to provide support. This might be through social programs, subsidies, or stimulus packages. These actions help cushion the blow and keep our economy afloat."

He then talks about monetary policy, controlled by the central government. "When the government adjusts interest rates or prints more money, they're trying to control inflation and stabilize the economy. Lower interest rates can encourage borrowing and spending, while higher rates can help cool down an overheated economy."

Finally, Kato covers international trade policies. "Our government negotiates trade agreements with other countries. These agreements can open up markets for our goods, like copper and crops, boosting our local economy. But they can also bring in competition. It's a delicate balance."

As Kato finishes, he sees the thoughtful expressions on the faces around him. People begin to discuss how these governmental roles have impacted their lives, from the subsidies that helped their farms survive a drought to the new school that has given their children hope for a brighter future.

An elderly man raises his hand. "Kato, how can we make sure our government acts in our best interest?"

Kato smiles, heartened by the question. "We need to stay informed and engaged. Attend community meetings, vote in elections, and hold our leaders accountable. By understanding the government's role and advocating for policies that benefit our community, we can help guide the hands that shape our economy."

As the session ends, Kato feels a sense of fulfillment. He has illuminated the crucial role of government in economic affairs, empowering his neighbors with the knowledge to engage actively in their community's economic decisions. Walking home, he feels a renewed sense of hope for Ndola's future, confident that an informed and active citizenry can drive meaningful change.

2

Chapter 2: Markets and Competition

Supply and Demand Dynamics

"The Heartbeat of Commerce: Exploring Supply and Demand Dynamics in Ndola"

The sun sets over Ndola, casting a golden hue over the bustling market. Traders call out to potential customers, and the air is thick with the sounds of commerce. Kato stands at the edge of the market, a familiar place that has come to symbolize the economic heartbeat of his community. Tonight, he is here to dramatize the principle of supply and demand dynamics, showing how these fundamental forces shape the lives of Ndola's residents.

Kato gathers a small group of curious onlookers near a popular vegetable stall. He greets the vendor, Mama Chanda, known for her fresh tomatoes. "Good evening, Mama Chanda," Kato says warmly. "Tonight, we're going to see how supply and demand affect your business."

Mama Chanda nods, smiling. She places a basket of tomatoes in front of her stall. "These tomatoes are the best in the market. Freshly picked this morning."

Kato turns to the crowd. "Let's imagine it's the peak of the harvest season. The fields are full, and every farmer is bringing their tomatoes to market. This means we have a high supply of tomatoes."

He motions to Mama Chanda, who adds more tomatoes to the display. "With so many tomatoes available, how do you think the prices will be?" he asks the crowd.

A young man steps forward. "They'll be lower because there's plenty of them."

"Exactly," Kato says. "When supply is high, prices tend to drop because there's more competition among sellers. Everyone is trying to sell their tomatoes, so they lower prices to attract buyers."

Mama Chanda nods, lowering the price on her sign. "I need to sell these quickly before they spoil," she explains.

Kato then shifts the scenario. "Now, let's imagine it's the dry season. There's a drought, and the tomato harvest is poor. Fewer tomatoes make it to the market, so the supply is low."

Mama Chanda removes most of the tomatoes from her stall, leaving only a few. "With so few tomatoes, what happens to the prices?" Kato asks.

An elderly woman chimes in. "The prices go up because everyone still wants tomatoes, but there aren't enough to go around."

Kato nods. "Exactly. When supply is low but demand remains high, prices increase. This is the basic principle of supply and demand at work."

He then introduces a twist. "What if a new farmer starts

bringing in a large amount of tomatoes, even during the dry season, because they have access to irrigation?"

Mama Chanda adds another basket of tomatoes to her stall, representing the new farmer's supply. The crowd murmurs as they see the increased supply.

"With more tomatoes available, even in the dry season, what happens to the prices?" Kato asks.

"They go down again," a young woman says. "There's more competition."

Kato smiles. "Exactly. The market adjusts based on supply and demand. Prices reflect the availability of goods and the desire of buyers to purchase them."

He turns back to the crowd. "Understanding these dynamics helps us make better decisions. As sellers, we can plan when to bring our goods to market for the best prices. As buyers, we can choose the best times to purchase what we need."

Mama Chanda nods in agreement. "And as a community, we can work together to stabilize our market, maybe through cooperatives or better storage facilities to manage supply."

Kato concludes the lesson, seeing the recognition and understanding in the eyes of his neighbors. "The forces of supply and demand are powerful, but with knowledge and cooperation, we can navigate them to our advantage."

As the crowd disperses, Kato feels a deep sense of accomplishment. He has illuminated the heartbeat of commerce, empowering his community with the knowledge to harness the dynamics of supply and demand. Walking home, he envisions a more informed and resilient Ndola, where the market's rhythms are understood and embraced by all.

Market Structures and Competition

"Fields of Competition: Understanding Market Structures in Ndola"

The bustling market of Ndola is alive with activity as Kato prepares for his next lesson. He stands near the center of the marketplace, ready to demonstrate the various market structures and how they influence competition. A diverse group of vendors and customers gathers, curious to learn more about the forces shaping their economic environment.

Kato starts by addressing the crowd. "Good evening, everyone. Tonight, we're going to explore different market structures and how they impact competition among businesses. Let's dive into how markets can vary and what that means for us as consumers and entrepreneurs."

He points to the vegetable vendors, including Mama Chanda. "Let's start with perfect competition. Imagine there are many vendors like Mama Chanda here, all selling similar tomatoes. None of them can set the price because there are so many options for buyers. This is a market with perfect competition."

Mama Chanda laughs. "I have to make sure my tomatoes are the best quality and priced right, or my customers will go to someone else."

Kato nods. "Exactly. In perfect competition, no single seller has control over the market. Prices are determined by supply and demand, and sellers must be efficient and competitive."

Next, Kato moves to the lone electronics stall run by a man named Mr. Mwansa. "Now, let's look at a monopoly. Imagine Mr. Mwansa is the only one selling solar chargers in all of Ndola. Because he has no competition, he can set higher prices."

Mr. Mwansa grins sheepishly. "If I were the only seller, I could charge more because people would have no other options."

"That's right," Kato says. "In a monopoly, a single seller controls the market, which can lead to higher prices and less choice for consumers."

He then points to a group of three mobile phone vendors. "Next, we have oligopoly, where a few sellers dominate the market. Imagine these three vendors control most of the mobile phone sales in Ndola. They might compete on prices and features, but they also have significant influence over the market."

One of the vendors, a woman named Zola, speaks up. "We watch each other's prices closely. If one of us lowers prices, the others have to follow or risk losing customers."

Kato nods. "Exactly. In an oligopoly, a few firms have considerable market power, and their actions are interdependent. They must be strategic in their decisions, as changes by one can impact the others."

He moves on to another example. "Now, let's talk about monopolistic competition. This is like our clothing market, where many sellers offer different styles and brands. Each vendor has some control over their prices because their products are unique."

A clothing vendor, Mrs. Kunda, chimes in. "People come to me for my unique designs. I can charge a bit more because they can't find the same clothes elsewhere."

"Correct," Kato says. "In monopolistic competition, businesses differentiate their products to attract customers. This differentiation gives them some pricing power, unlike in perfect competition."

Finally, Kato introduces a new concept. "Let's consider a theoretical structure called perfect monopoly, where there's only one seller in the market, but it's regulated by the government to ensure fair prices and quality."

He turns to the crowd. "Imagine if Mr. Mwansa's solar chargers were the only option, but the government set the prices to make sure they were affordable and the products were high quality. This can happen in industries like utilities, where natural monopolies exist."

As Kato finishes, the crowd buzzes with conversation, applying these concepts to their own experiences and businesses. They begin to see how understanding market structures can help them navigate the economic landscape, whether they are buyers seeking the best deals or sellers aiming to position their products effectively.

An elderly woman raises her hand. "Kato, how can we use this knowledge to improve our market here in Ndola?"

Kato smiles, encouraged by the question. "We can encourage fair competition by supporting local entrepreneurs, advocating for regulations that prevent monopolistic practices, and promoting product diversity to give consumers more choices. By understanding market structures, we can create a more vibrant and competitive marketplace."

As the crowd disperses, Kato feels a sense of accomplishment. He has unveiled the complexities of market structures and competition, empowering his community with the knowledge to enhance their economic environment. Walking home, he imagines a future where Ndola's market thrives with fair competition, innovation, and prosperity for all.

Pricing Mechanisms in Modern Markets

"The Price is Right: Unveiling Pricing Mechanisms in Modern Markets in Ndola"

The marketplace in Ndola is a hive of activity as vendors set up their stalls, and customers browse for the best deals. Amidst the vibrant scene, Kato stands ready to educate his community on a crucial aspect of economics: pricing mechanisms in modern markets. Tonight, he aims to demystify how prices are determined and how different factors influence these mechanisms.

Kato gathers a diverse group of vendors and customers around a central area. "Good evening, everyone," he begins with a smile. "Tonight, we're going to talk about how prices are set in modern markets. Understanding these mechanisms will help us make smarter decisions as both buyers and sellers."

He starts with a simple example using Mama Chanda's tomatoes. "Let's say Mama Chanda wants to set the price for her tomatoes. How does she decide the right price?"

Mama Chanda thinks for a moment. "I look at what others are charging and how much it costs me to grow and bring them here."

"That's right," Kato says. "This is called cost-plus pricing. Mama Chanda calculates her costs and adds a markup to ensure she makes a profit. It's a common method, especially for small businesses."

He then addresses dynamic pricing. "Imagine it's a holiday, and lots of people are buying tomatoes for celebrations. Mama Chanda might raise her prices because the demand is higher."

A young man in the crowd speaks up. "Like how bus fares

CHAPTER 2: MARKETS AND COMPETITION

go up during festive seasons."

"Exactly," Kato nods. "That's dynamic pricing. Prices fluctuate based on demand. Businesses use it to maximize profits when demand is high and adjust when demand is low."

Kato shifts to another example. "Now, let's talk about penetration pricing. When a new vendor enters the market, they might set lower prices to attract customers and build a base. Once they have loyal customers, they can gradually increase prices."

Zola, the mobile phone vendor, chimes in. "I did that when I first started selling phones. It helped me get noticed."

"Precisely," Kato says. "Penetration pricing is effective for new businesses trying to establish themselves in a competitive market."

Next, he explains price discrimination. "This is when a business charges different prices to different groups of customers. For instance, a bus company might charge lower fares for students and seniors."

An elderly woman nods. "Yes, I get a discount on my bus fare because of my age."

"That's price discrimination," Kato confirms. "It allows businesses to cater to different customer segments and maximize their overall revenue."

He then touches on psychological pricing. "Have you ever noticed how prices are often set at K99 instead of K100? That's psychological pricing. It makes prices seem lower and more attractive to buyers."

Mama Chanda laughs. "I've seen that! It does make things seem cheaper."

Kato smiles. "It's a simple but effective technique. Businesses use it to encourage purchases by making prices appear more appealing."

Finally, Kato discusses competitive pricing. "In a market with many sellers, like our vegetable market, businesses often set their prices based on what their competitors charge. This helps them stay competitive and attract customers."

Mrs. Kunda, the clothing vendor, nods. "I always check what others are charging before setting my prices."

"That's a smart strategy," Kato says. "Competitive pricing ensures you remain attractive to customers while staying in line with market rates."

As Kato concludes, the crowd begins to discuss how these pricing mechanisms affect their daily transactions and businesses. They start brainstorming ways to implement these strategies to improve their sales and make better purchasing decisions.

A young entrepreneur raises his hand. "Kato, how can we use this knowledge to make our market more efficient?"

Kato responds thoughtfully. "By understanding these pricing mechanisms, we can set fair and strategic prices that reflect true value and demand. As buyers, we can recognize when prices are fair and make informed choices. This knowledge empowers us all to create a more balanced and thriving market."

As the crowd disperses, Kato feels a sense of fulfillment. He has shed light on the intricate workings of pricing mechanisms, equipping his community with the tools to navigate the modern market landscape. Walking home, he envisions a marketplace in Ndola where informed sellers and savvy buyers thrive together, creating a robust and dynamic local economy.

Market Failures and Externalities

"Beyond the Market: Tackling Market Failures and Externalities in Ndola"

The community center in Ndola is filled with curious residents, eager to learn from Kato's next lesson. Tonight's topic is complex but vital for understanding the full picture of economics: market failures and externalities. Kato knows that explaining these concepts will help his community identify and address the unintended consequences of market activities.

Kato stands before the assembled group, ready to bring these abstract concepts to life. "Good evening, everyone. Tonight, we're discussing something crucial—what happens when markets don't work as they should and the hidden effects of our economic activities."

He begins with a relatable scenario. "Let's imagine a factory opens near our village, producing goods that we all need. This factory creates jobs and boosts our economy. But what if this factory also pollutes our river?"

The crowd murmurs, recognizing the problem immediately. "Our water would be contaminated," a woman named Grace says. "We'd have to find other sources of water, and it might make us sick."

"Exactly," Kato says. "This is an example of a negative externality. The factory's pollution is an unintended side effect that affects everyone, not just those who work there or buy its products."

He explains further. "Externalities are costs or benefits that affect others who did not choose to be involved in the economic transaction. Negative externalities, like pollution, impose costs on the community."

Kato turns to the concept of market failures. "Market failures occur when the free market doesn't allocate resources efficiently on its own. Pollution is one cause, but there are others."

He points to a recent example in Ndola. "Remember the cholera outbreak last year? It spread because some areas lacked proper sanitation, which is a public good."

An elderly man named Mwansa speaks up. "The government had to step in to provide clean water and sanitation facilities."

"Exactly," Kato nods. "Public goods, like clean water and sanitation, are often underprovided by the market because everyone benefits from them, and it's hard to charge people directly. This is a market failure, and government intervention is necessary to provide these goods."

He moves on to another example. "Think about healthcare. If only the wealthy can afford it, the poor get sicker and can't work, which affects the whole economy. This is another type of market failure."

A young mother named Alice adds, "When my daughter was sick, we struggled to afford her treatment. It affected our entire family."

Kato nods sympathetically. "Healthcare is a merit good—everyone benefits from it, but not everyone can afford it. The government or charities often need to step in to ensure everyone has access."

To illustrate positive externalities, Kato gives another example. "Let's consider education. When more people in our community are educated, we all benefit from a more knowledgeable and skilled workforce."

Grace smiles. "My son's education has helped him get a good job, which benefits our whole family."

"Exactly," Kato says. "Education creates positive externalities. The benefits extend beyond the individual to society as a whole."

He explains how governments can correct market failures and manage externalities. "The government can impose regulations to limit pollution, provide public goods like clean water, and subsidize services like healthcare and education to ensure everyone has access."

Kato concludes by encouraging the community to think about their role. "As citizens, we need to advocate for policies that address these issues. We must support regulations that protect our environment and ensure everyone has access to essential services."

The crowd buzzes with conversation, discussing how these concepts apply to their own experiences. They start to see the connections between their daily lives and the broader economic principles Kato has explained.

A young man raises his hand. "Kato, what can we do as a community to help address these market failures?"

Kato smiles. "We can start by raising awareness, supporting local initiatives that promote clean water, education, and healthcare, and working together to hold businesses and government accountable for their impacts on our community."

As the session ends, Kato feels a deep sense of accomplishment. He has illuminated the hidden forces of market failures and externalities, empowering his community to recognize and address these challenges. Walking home, he envisions a more informed and proactive Ndola, where the community works together to create a fairer and more sustainable economy.

The Economics of Information

"The Power of Knowledge: Unraveling the Economics of Information in Ndola"

The evening air in Ndola is crisp as Kato gathers the community for another insightful session at the community center. Tonight, he plans to shed light on a vital but often overlooked aspect of economics: the economics of information. Understanding how information shapes markets and decision-making is crucial for the people of Ndola to thrive in the modern economy.

Kato stands before the attentive crowd, a mix of vendors, farmers, and local residents. "Good evening, everyone. Tonight, we're going to explore the economics of information. Information is a powerful tool in the marketplace, and understanding how it works can help us make better decisions."

He begins with a simple, relatable example. "Imagine you're buying a used bicycle. One seller tells you the bike is in excellent condition, while another doesn't say anything about its state. Who would you trust more?"

A young man named Joseph raises his hand. "I'd trust the seller who tells me about the condition. It shows they're being honest."

"Exactly," Kato says. "This is an example of information asymmetry. When one party has more or better information than the other, it can lead to imbalances and potentially unfair transactions."

Kato moves to another example. "Think about our farmers

CHAPTER 2: MARKETS AND COMPETITION

here. If some farmers have access to information about better seeds and farming techniques, while others do not, what happens?"

Mama Chanda, always engaged in the discussions, speaks up. "Those with better information will have higher yields and make more money."

"Correct," Kato says. "Information asymmetry can create disparities in income and opportunities. But if everyone had access to the same information, we'd see more equal benefits across our community."

He explains how information affects market decisions. "Consider the stock market. Investors make decisions based on available information about companies. If some investors have inside information that others don't, they can make profits at the expense of others. This is why regulations exist to ensure transparency and fairness."

A young woman named Lydia asks, "How can we make sure everyone gets the right information?"

"Great question," Kato replies. "There are several ways. One is through education and training programs that share valuable knowledge and skills. Another is transparency from businesses and institutions, ensuring they provide accurate information to the public."

He highlights the role of technology. "With the rise of the internet and mobile phones, information has become more accessible. Farmers can check market prices, weather forecasts, and new farming techniques online, helping them make better decisions."

An elderly man named Mwansa nods. "I've seen younger farmers using their phones to get information about crop diseases and treatments. It's impressive."

"Indeed," Kato says. "Access to information can level the playing field and empower individuals to improve their livelihoods. But we must also be wary of misinformation and ensure we use reliable sources."

He introduces the concept of signaling. "Sometimes, businesses use signals to convey information. For example, a farmer might get a certification to show their produce is organic. This signal helps buyers trust the quality of the product."

Mama Chanda nods thoughtfully. "That's like when I tell my customers my tomatoes are from my pesticide-free farm. It helps build trust."

"Exactly," Kato smiles. "Signaling helps reduce information asymmetry and builds trust between buyers and sellers."

Kato wraps up with a discussion on adverse selection and moral hazard. "In insurance markets, adverse selection occurs when those most likely to make claims are the ones who buy insurance, driving up costs. Moral hazard happens when insured individuals take more risks because they know they're protected."

Lydia frowns. "So, how do insurers manage these problems?"

"Insurers use screening and incentives to manage these risks," Kato explains. "They gather information about applicants to assess risk levels and offer incentives for safe behavior, like lower premiums for safe drivers."

As the session concludes, the crowd is abuzz with newfound understanding. They discuss how access to better information could transform their businesses and lives.

A farmer raises his hand. "Kato, how can we make sure everyone in Ndola gets the information they need?"

Kato smiles, heartened by the proactive question. "We can create information-sharing networks, hold regular community workshops, and advocate for better access to technology and education. By working together, we can ensure everyone benefits from the wealth of information available."

As the community disperses, Kato feels a profound sense of achievement. He has illuminated the critical role of information in the economy, empowering his neighbors to harness its power for better decision-making. Walking home, he envisions a future where Ndola thrives on the shared knowledge, ensuring prosperity and equality for all.

Globalization and Market Integration

"Bridging Worlds: Understanding Globalization and Market Integration in Ndola"

The community center in Ndola is bustling with excitement as Kato prepares to conclude his series on markets and competition with a discussion on globalization and market integration. This topic is particularly relevant as the residents of Ndola experience the effects of global markets on their local economy. Kato aims to demystify how global connections shape their daily lives and economic opportunities.

Kato stands at the front of the room, facing a crowd eager to understand the global forces at play. "Good evening, everyone. Tonight, we're going to explore how globalization and market integration affect us right here in Ndola. These forces connect us to the rest of the world in ways we might not always realize."

He starts with a simple example. "Look at the clothes we wear, the phones we use, and even some of the food we eat.

Many of these items come from other countries. This is globalization at work—goods and services moving across borders, creating a global marketplace."

Mama Chanda, a familiar face in the crowd, raises her hand. "I've noticed the prices of imported goods changing frequently. Why does that happen?"

"Great observation," Kato replies. "Prices fluctuate due to changes in global supply and demand, currency exchange rates, and international trade policies. For example, if a drought affects crops in another country, the price of those imported goods might rise here."

He continues with a local perspective. "Our own market in Ndola is influenced by these global changes. Think about the copper mines nearby. Copper is a significant export for Zambia, and its price is determined on the global market. When global demand for copper increases, it benefits our local economy."

A young man named Joseph speaks up. "But what about local businesses? How do they compete with imported goods?"

"That's a key challenge," Kato says. "Globalization can bring competition from foreign products, which might be cheaper or perceived as higher quality. Local businesses need to innovate and find ways to differentiate their products to compete effectively."

He introduces the concept of market integration. "Market integration happens when markets around the world become interconnected. This can lead to more efficient resource allocation, access to a broader range of goods and services, and greater economic growth."

A young woman named Lydia asks, "How does market integration affect jobs here in Ndola?"

"Good question," Kato responds. "Market integration can create new job opportunities by attracting foreign investment and opening new markets for our goods. However, it can also lead to job losses in industries that struggle to compete with imported goods. It's important for workers to adapt and acquire new skills to thrive in a changing economy."

Kato then explains the role of trade agreements. "Trade agreements between countries reduce barriers to trade, such as tariffs and quotas, making it easier for goods and services to move across borders. Zambia is part of several regional trade agreements that help integrate our market with neighboring countries."

Mwansa, an elderly man in the crowd, nods thoughtfully. "I've seen more goods from neighboring countries at our market. It's good to have more options, but sometimes our local products are overlooked."

"That's a valid point," Kato says. "Trade agreements can bring benefits, but it's also essential to support our local industries. This can be done through government policies that promote local businesses and encourage exports."

He concludes by emphasizing the importance of adaptability. "In a globalized world, it's crucial for our community to stay informed and adaptable. Embracing new technologies, learning new skills, and staying competitive can help us harness the benefits of globalization while mitigating its challenges."

The crowd begins to discuss how globalization has affected their own lives and businesses. They share stories of imported goods, fluctuating prices, and new opportunities.

A young entrepreneur raises her hand. "Kato, how can we ensure that globalization benefits our community?"

Kato smiles, encouraged by the proactive question. "We can start by supporting local businesses, advocating for fair trade practices, and investing in education and skills development. By staying informed and adaptable, we can navigate the challenges of globalization and seize its opportunities."

As the session ends, the crowd disperses with a deeper understanding of the global forces at play and their impact on Ndola. Kato feels a sense of fulfillment, knowing he has equipped his community with the knowledge to navigate the complexities of globalization and market integration. Walking home, he envisions a future where Ndola thrives as a dynamic part of the global economy, with informed and empowered citizens leading the way.

3

Chapter 3: Labor and Human Capital

The Economics of Labor Markets

"Empowering Work: Exploring the Economics of Labor Markets in Ndola"

In the heart of Ndola, where the rhythm of life pulses through the bustling streets, Kato gathers the community once again, this time to delve into the intricate world of labor and human capital. The session is charged with anticipation as Kato prepares to unravel the economics of labor markets, a topic that resonates deeply with the residents of Ndola, where the toil of labor sustains families and fuels dreams of prosperity.

Kato stands before the eager crowd, his voice resonating with warmth and determination. "Good evening, everyone. Tonight, we embark on a journey to understand the economics of labor markets—where the tireless efforts of our workers intersect with the forces of supply and demand, shaping the fabric of our community."

He begins with a vivid illustration. "Imagine a young woman named Mary, a skilled tailor who stitches together the fabric of our community. Mary's labor is not just a means of survival—it is the essence of her identity, the foundation of her dreams."

The crowd nods in understanding, their faces reflecting the shared experiences of labor and livelihood.

"Yet," Kato continues, "the value of Mary's labor is not fixed. It fluctuates with the ebb and flow of the labor market—where supply meets demand."

He points to the vendors in the market, the farmers toiling in the fields, and the artisans crafting their wares. "Each worker, each laborer, contributes to the tapestry of our economy. But their wages, their livelihoods, are determined by the forces of the labor market."

Kato explains the concept of supply and demand in labor markets. "When demand for workers is high—perhaps due to a construction boom or a surge in agricultural production—employers compete for labor, driving wages up. Conversely, when demand is low, wages may stagnate or even decline."

He then addresses the role of human capital. "Human capital—the skills, knowledge, and experience that workers possess—is the bedrock of our labor market. Just as a carpenter hones their craft, or a teacher shares their wisdom, human capital enriches our community and fuels economic growth."

A young man named Daniel raises his hand. "But what about unemployment? Why do some people struggle to find work?"

"Ah, an astute question," Kato replies. "Unemployment, whether due to technological shifts, economic downturns, or structural barriers, can cast a shadow over our community.

CHAPTER 3: LABOR AND HUMAN CAPITAL

It highlights the need for policies and programs that support job creation, skill development, and equal opportunities for all."

He then addresses the concept of labor mobility. "In a dynamic labor market, workers must be able to adapt to changing conditions. Whether seeking better opportunities in neighboring towns or migrating to urban centers, labor mobility is essential for economic resilience and growth."

Kato concludes by emphasizing the importance of fair labor practices. "As a community, we must champion fair wages, safe working conditions, and equal opportunities for all. By valuing the dignity of labor, we build a stronger, more inclusive society."

As the session draws to a close, the crowd is abuzz with discussion, sharing their insights and experiences. They reflect on the challenges and opportunities of the labor market, and the pivotal role it plays in shaping their lives.

A seasoned farmer named Elijah speaks up. "Kato, how can we ensure that our labor market works for everyone?"

Kato smiles, inspired by the collective spirit of his community. "By advocating for policies that promote job creation, investing in education and skills development, and fostering a culture of innovation and entrepreneurship, we can unlock the full potential of our labor force. Together, we can build a future where every worker thrives and every dream finds its wings."

As the crowd disperses, Kato feels a profound sense of fulfillment. He has illuminated the complexities of labor markets, empowering his community with the knowledge to navigate their economic futures with confidence and resilience. Walking home, he envisions a Ndola where the dignity of labor is honored, and the promise of prosperity is within reach for all.

Wage Determination and Labor Mobility

"Pathways to Prosperity: Unraveling Wage Determination and Labor Mobility in Ndola"

In the heart of Ndola, where the beat of the city echoes the rhythm of life, Kato returns to the community center, ready to illuminate the intricacies of wage determination and labor mobility. The anticipation in the air is palpable as the residents gather, eager to understand how their wages are set and how they can navigate the pathways of opportunity in the dynamic labor market.

Kato stands before the crowd, his voice a beacon of clarity in the sea of eager faces. "Good evening, friends. Tonight, we embark on a journey to uncover the mysteries of wage determination and labor mobility—two pillars that shape the landscape of our economic lives."

He begins with a simple yet profound question. "How are wages determined? What sets the value of our labor?"

The crowd leans in, captivated by Kato's words.

"Wages," Kato explains, "are not arbitrary. They are the result of a delicate dance between supply and demand in the labor market."

He gestures to the vendors in the market, the artisans crafting their wares, and the workers toiling in the fields. "When demand for labor is high—perhaps due to a booming industry or a seasonal surge in production—employers compete for workers, driving wages up. Conversely, when demand is low,

CHAPTER 3: LABOR AND HUMAN CAPITAL

wages may stagnate or even decline."

A young woman named Fatima raises her hand. "But how do we know if we're being paid fairly? Is there a standard?"

Kato nods, acknowledging the importance of fairness in wage determination. "Indeed, Fatima. While there may not be a universal standard, factors such as skill level, experience, and the prevailing market conditions all play a role in determining wages. It's essential for workers to advocate for fair compensation and to seek opportunities for advancement."

He then turns his attention to labor mobility. "In a dynamic economy, labor mobility is the lifeblood of opportunity. Whether seeking better wages in neighboring towns or pursuing new career paths in urban centers, the ability to move and adapt is essential for economic resilience and growth."

A farmer named John speaks up. "But what about those of us who can't afford to move? How can we access better opportunities?"

Kato's expression softens with empathy. "Ah, an important question, John. While physical mobility is one aspect, there are other pathways to prosperity. Investing in education and skills development, fostering entrepreneurship, and creating supportive community networks are all ways to unlock opportunities right here at home."

He then shares stories of individuals who have overcome adversity through resilience and determination. "Take Mama Chanda, for example," Kato says, gesturing to the revered vendor in the market. "Through hard work and innovation, she transformed her small vegetable stall into a thriving business, providing employment for others in the process."

Mama Chanda smiles, her eyes shining with pride.

Kato concludes by emphasizing the power of collective

action. "As a community, we must advocate for policies that promote fair wages, support skill development, and create an environment where everyone has the opportunity to thrive. Together, we can forge a path to prosperity for all."

As the session draws to a close, the crowd is abuzz with conversation, sharing their aspirations and exchanging ideas for building a brighter future. With newfound clarity and resolve, they disperse into the night, ready to chart their own paths in the dynamic landscape of the labor market.

Kato watches them go, a sense of pride swelling in his heart. He knows that with knowledge and determination, the residents of Ndola can overcome any obstacle and forge a future filled with opportunity and prosperity.

Education and Skills Development

"Building Bridges to Tomorrow: Nurturing Education and Skills Development in Ndola"

As the sun sets over Ndola, illuminating the horizon with hues of gold and crimson, Kato returns to the community center, ready to unveil the transformative power of education and skills development. The air is charged with anticipation as the residents gather once again, eager to explore the pathways to knowledge and opportunity that lie ahead.

Kato stands before the assembled crowd, his gaze alight with passion and purpose. "Good evening, my friends. Tonight, we embark on a journey to unlock the boundless potential of education and skills development—the keys to a brighter future for ourselves and our community."

He begins with a poignant reflection. "In the tapestry of life, education is the thread that binds us together, weaving dreams into reality and illuminating the pathways of possibility."

The crowd listens intently, captivated by Kato's words.

"Education," Kato explains, "is not merely the acquisition of knowledge, but the cultivation of skills, the nurturing of talents, and the awakening of potential within each of us."

He gestures to the children playing nearby, their eyes wide with curiosity. "From the youngest among us to the oldest, education knows no bounds. It is a lifelong journey of discovery and growth."

Kato then turns his attention to skills development. "In the ever-evolving landscape of the modern economy, skills are the currency of opportunity. Whether it be the mastery of a trade, the proficiency in a craft, or the expertise in a field of study, skills open doors to new horizons and brighter futures."

A young man named Samuel raises his hand. "But what if we lack access to education and skills training? How can we break free from the cycle of poverty?"

Kato's expression softens with empathy. "Ah, Samuel, a poignant question indeed. While the journey may be challenging, there are bridges we can build, pathways we can forge, to access the opportunities that lie beyond."

He shares stories of individuals who have overcome adversity through education and skills development. "Take Joseph, for example," Kato says, nodding to the young man in the crowd. "Through determination and perseverance, he pursued vocational training in carpentry, unlocking a world of opportunities in the construction industry."

Joseph beams with pride, his eyes shining with hope.

Kato then speaks of the importance of community support. "As a community, we must rally together to support education and skills development initiatives. Whether it be through mentorship programs, vocational training centers, or scholarships for higher education, we can nurture the talents and aspirations of our youth, ensuring a brighter future for generations to come."

He concludes with a call to action. "Let us embrace the power of education and skills development as instruments of change, catalysts of progress, and beacons of hope. Together, we can build a future where every individual has the opportunity to flourish and thrive."

As the session draws to a close, the crowd is filled with a renewed sense of purpose and determination. With newfound clarity and resolve, they disperse into the night, ready to embark on their own journeys of learning and growth.

Kato watches them go, his heart brimming with pride. He knows that with education as their compass and skills as their guide, the residents of Ndola can navigate any obstacle and forge a future filled with promise and possibility.

Unemployment and Underemployment

"Overcoming Obstacles: Confronting Unemployment and Underemployment in Ndola"

As twilight settles over Ndola, casting long shadows across the bustling streets, Kato returns to the community center, prepared to confront the stark realities of unemployment and underemployment. The air is heavy with a mix of concern and determination as the residents gather, ready to address the challenges that loom on the horizon.

Kato stands before the attentive crowd, his presence a

beacon of reassurance amidst the sea of worried faces. "Good evening, my friends. Tonight, we confront a formidable adversary—unemployment and underemployment. But fear not, for together, we shall face these challenges head-on, armed with the power of knowledge and community solidarity."

He begins with a somber reflection. "In the fabric of our society, unemployment and underemployment are threads of hardship, weaving a tapestry of uncertainty and despair. But let us not succumb to despair, for within each challenge lies an opportunity for growth and renewal."

The crowd listens intently, their eyes reflecting a mix of concern and hope.

"Unemployment," Kato explains, "is not merely the absence of work, but the erosion of dignity, the stifling of potential, and the fracture of dreams. It affects individuals, families, and communities, casting a shadow of uncertainty over our collective future."

He gestures to the vendors in the market, the artisans crafting their wares, and the workers toiling in the fields. "Yet amidst the hardship, there lies resilience—the resilience of a community united in solidarity, determined to forge a path to brighter tomorrows."

Kato then turns his attention to underemployment. "In the shadows of unemployment lurks underemployment—a silent specter that haunts our economy, trapping individuals in cycles of low-wage labor and limited opportunities for advancement."

A young woman named Esther raises her hand. "But how can we break free from the cycle of unemployment and underemployment? What steps can we take to create a future of prosperity for all?"

Kato's expression softens with empathy. "Ah, Esther, a question that weighs heavy on the hearts of many. While the journey may be arduous, there are pathways we can tread, bridges we can build, to transcend the barriers that stand in our way."

He shares stories of individuals who have overcome unemployment and underemployment through perseverance and resilience. "Take David, for example," Kato says, nodding to the young man in the crowd. "Despite facing numerous setbacks, he remained steadfast in his pursuit of opportunity, eventually finding success through entrepreneurship."

David smiles, his eyes shining with determination.

Kato then speaks of the importance of community support. "As a community, we must rally together to support those in need, offering assistance, guidance, and encouragement along their journey. Whether it be through job training programs, small business loans, or mentorship initiatives, we can empower individuals to break free from the chains of unemployment and underemployment."

He concludes with a call to action. "Let us rise, my friends, united in our determination to overcome adversity and create a future of prosperity for all. Together, we can transform the shadows of despair into beacons of hope, lighting the way to brighter tomorrows."

As the session draws to a close, the crowd is filled with a renewed sense of purpose and resolve. With determination in their hearts and solidarity in their souls, they disperse into the night, ready to face the challenges that lie ahead.

Kato watches them go, his heart swelling with pride. He knows that with unity as their shield and resilience as their armor, the residents of Ndola can conquer any obstacle and build a future filled with opportunity and prosperity.

Gender and Racial Disparities in the Labor Market

"Breaking Barriers: Addressing Gender and Racial Disparities in Ndola's Labor Market"

As the sun dips below the horizon, casting a warm glow over the city of Ndola, Kato returns to the community center, prepared to shine a light on the pervasive issues of gender and racial disparities in the labor market. The atmosphere is charged with a mix of determination and concern as the residents gather, ready to confront the systemic barriers that hinder equality and opportunity.

Kato stands before the assembled crowd, his voice a beacon of determination amidst the sea of attentive faces. "Good evening, my friends. Tonight, we confront an issue that strikes at the very heart of our community—the pervasive disparities of gender and race in the labor market. But fear not, for together, we shall embark on a journey of understanding and empowerment."

He begins with a solemn reflection. "In the tapestry of our society, gender and racial disparities are threads of injustice, weaving a fabric of inequality and exclusion. But let us not be deterred by the enormity of the challenge, for within each injustice lies an opportunity for change and progress."

The crowd listens intently, their expressions a mix of empathy and determination.

"Gender disparities," Kato explains, "are not merely statistics—they are lived experiences, echoing through the generations, shaping the destinies of women and girls in our community. From unequal pay to limited access to leadership roles, these disparities cast a shadow of injustice over our labor market."

He gestures to the women in the crowd, their faces reflecting the struggles and triumphs of generations past. "Yet amidst the adversity, there lies resilience—the resilience of women who have shattered glass ceilings, defied stereotypes, and carved out their own paths to success."

Kato then turns his attention to racial disparities. "In a diverse community like ours, racial disparities are wounds that run deep, scars of discrimination and prejudice that mar the landscape of opportunity. From unequal access to education to systemic barriers in hiring and promotion, these disparities perpetuate cycles of inequality and exclusion."

A young man named Elias raises his hand. "But how can we dismantle these barriers? What steps can we take to create a more inclusive and equitable labor market?"

Kato's expression softens with empathy. "Ah, Elias, a question that weighs heavy on the hearts of many. While the journey may be fraught with challenges, there are paths we can tread, bridges we can build, to dismantle the barriers that stand in our way."

He shares stories of individuals who have overcome gender and racial disparities through resilience and determination. "Take Sarah, for example," Kato says, nodding to the young woman in the crowd. "Despite facing discrimination in the workplace, she remained steadfast in her pursuit of equality, eventually becoming a champion for diversity and inclusion in our community."

Sarah smiles, her eyes shining with pride.

Kato then speaks of the importance of community support. "As a community, we must rally together to dismantle systemic barriers and foster a culture of equality and inclusion. Whether it be through advocacy, education, or mentorship, we can empower individuals to break free from the chains of discrimination and pursue their dreams without fear or prejudice."

He concludes with a call to action. "Let us rise, my friends, united in our determination to break down barriers and build a future where every individual—regardless of gender or race—has the opportunity to thrive and succeed."

As the session draws to a close, the crowd is filled with a renewed sense of purpose and resolve. With solidarity in their hearts and justice in their sights, they disperse into the night, ready to confront the systemic injustices that linger in the shadows of their community.

Kato watches them go, his heart swelling with pride. He knows that with determination as their guide and unity as their strength, the residents of Ndola can overcome any obstacle and build a future where equality and opportunity reign supreme.

Technological Innovation and the Future of Work

"Embracing Change: Navigating Technological Innovation and the Future of Work in Ndola"

As the city of Ndola hums with the energy of a new day, Kato returns to the community center, ready to explore the transformative power of technological innovation and its impact on the future of work. The atmosphere crackles with anticipation as the residents gather, eager to understand how they can adapt and thrive in an ever-evolving economic landscape.

Kato stands before the assembled crowd, his presence a beacon of hope amidst the sea of eager faces. "Good morning, my friends. Today, we embark on a journey to unravel the mysteries of technological innovation and its profound implications for the future of work in our beloved Ndola. But fear not, for together, we shall navigate these uncharted waters with courage and resilience."

He begins with a contemplative reflection. "In the tapestry of our society, technological innovation is a thread of change—a force that reshapes industries, redefines roles, and revolutionizes the way we work. But let us not be daunted by the magnitude of this transformation, for within each challenge lies an opportunity for adaptation and growth."

The crowd listens intently, their expressions a mix of curiosity and apprehension.

"Technological innovation," Kato explains, "is not merely the advent of new tools and technologies—it is a catalyst for progress, a harbinger of efficiency, and a driver of economic growth. From automation to artificial intelligence, these innovations hold the promise of unlocking new possibilities and unleashing human potential."

CHAPTER 3: LABOR AND HUMAN CAPITAL

He gestures to the young people in the crowd, their faces illuminated with excitement for the future. "Yet amidst the uncertainty, there lies opportunity—the opportunity to embrace change, to acquire new skills, and to seize the reins of innovation in our own hands."

Kato then turns his attention to the future of work. "In a world shaped by technological innovation, the landscape of employment is shifting—a kaleidoscope of new opportunities, new challenges, and new frontiers. From remote work to gig economy platforms, the ways in which we work are evolving at an unprecedented pace."

A middle-aged woman named Rebecca raises her hand. "But what about those of us who may be left behind by these changes? How can we adapt and thrive in a world that seems to move faster than we can keep up?"

Kato's expression softens with empathy. "Ah, Rebecca, a question that weighs heavy on the hearts of many. While the journey may be fraught with uncertainty, there are pathways we can tread, bridges we can build, to navigate the challenges that lie ahead."

He shares stories of individuals who have embraced technological innovation and found success in the changing landscape of work. "Take James, for example," Kato says, nodding to the young man in the crowd. "Despite facing challenges in traditional employment, he leveraged his skills and creativity to launch a successful online business, tapping into global markets and forging a path to prosperity."

James smiles, his eyes shining with pride.

Kato then speaks of the importance of lifelong learning. "In a world where knowledge is power, education is the compass that guides us forward. Whether it be through upskilling programs, vocational training, or online courses, we must embrace a culture of lifelong learning to stay ahead of the curve and seize the opportunities that lie on the horizon."

He concludes with a call to action. "Let us rise, my friends, united in our determination to embrace change, to adapt and thrive in a world shaped by technological innovation. Together, we can harness the power of innovation to build a future where every individual has the opportunity to flourish and succeed."

As the session draws to a close, the crowd is filled with a renewed sense of optimism and determination. With resilience in their hearts and innovation in their minds, they disperse into the dawn, ready to embrace the challenges and opportunities of a future filled with promise and possibility.

Kato watches them go, his heart swelling with pride. He knows that with courage as their compass and adaptability as their strength, the residents of Ndola can navigate any obstacle and build a future where innovation and progress reign supreme.

4

Chapter 4: Money, Banking, and Monetary Policy

The Functions of Money

"Navigating the Currency of Change: Exploring Money, Banking, and Monetary Policy in Ndola"

In the heart of Ndola, where the rhythm of life pulses through the bustling streets, Kato returns to the community center, prepared to delve into the complexities of money, banking, and monetary policy. The air is charged with anticipation as the residents gather, eager to unravel the mysteries of finance that shape their daily lives.

Kato stands before the attentive crowd, his voice a beacon of clarity amidst the sea of curious faces. "Good evening, my friends. Tonight, we embark on a journey to explore the fundamental concepts of money—the lifeblood of our economy, the currency of change. But fear not, for together, we shall demystify these concepts and unlock the secrets of financial literacy."

He begins with a thought-provoking reflection. "In the tapestry of our society, money is more than mere currency—it is a symbol of trust, a medium of exchange, and a store of value. But let us not be blinded by its simplicity, for within the functions of money lie the foundations of our economic prosperity."

The crowd listens intently, their faces reflecting a mix of curiosity and intrigue.

"Money," Kato explains, "serves three primary functions: as a medium of exchange, a unit of account, and a store of value. Together, these functions form the cornerstone of our economic transactions, facilitating trade, measuring value, and preserving wealth."

He gestures to the marketplace nearby, where vendors exchange goods and services with eager customers. "As a medium of exchange, money enables us to conduct transactions with ease and efficiency, eliminating the need for cumbersome barter systems and fostering specialization and trade."

Kato then turns his attention to the concept of a unit of account. "In addition to facilitating transactions, money serves as a unit of account—a common measure of value that allows us to compare the worth of different goods and services. Whether it be the price of a loaf of bread or the cost of a haircut, money provides a universal standard for assessing value."

A young man named Daniel raises his hand. "But what about inflation? How does it affect the value of money and our ability to make informed decisions?"

Kato's expression softens with empathy. "Ah, Daniel, an astute question indeed. While inflation can erode the purchasing power of money over time, it also reflects the dynamics of supply and demand in the economy. By understanding inflation and its causes, we can make informed decisions to protect and grow our wealth."

He then speaks of money as a store of value. "Finally, money serves as a store of value—a means of preserving wealth and purchasing power over time. Whether it be through savings accounts, investments, or other financial instruments, money allows us to accumulate assets and plan for the future."

Kato concludes with a call to action. "Let us embrace the power of financial literacy as a tool for empowerment and economic resilience. By understanding the functions of money, we can make informed decisions, navigate the complexities of the financial system, and build a future of prosperity for ourselves and our community."

As the session draws to a close, the crowd is filled with a renewed sense of understanding and empowerment. With clarity in their minds and confidence in their hearts, they disperse into the night, ready to apply their newfound knowledge to their everyday lives.

Kato watches them go, his heart swelling with pride. He knows that with financial literacy as their guide, the residents of Ndola can navigate the currents of change and build a future where prosperity knows no bounds.

Banking Institutions and Financial Intermediation

"Building Bridges of Trust: Exploring Banking Institutions and Financial Intermediation in Ndola"

As the sun rises over Ndola, casting a golden glow over the city, Kato returns to the community center, prepared to delve deeper into the world of finance. The air is filled with a sense of anticipation as the residents gather once again, eager to unravel the mysteries of banking institutions and financial intermediation.

Kato stands before the attentive crowd, his voice carrying the weight of knowledge and wisdom. "Good morning, my friends. Today, we continue our journey into the realm of finance, exploring the vital role of banking institutions and financial intermediation in our economy. But fear not, for together, we shall navigate these waters with clarity and understanding."

He begins with a reflective tone. "In the tapestry of our society, banking institutions are the pillars of trust, the guardians of financial stability, and the engines of economic growth. But let us not be blinded by their grandeur, for within the halls of these institutions lie the hopes and dreams of our community."

The crowd listens intently, their faces reflecting a mix of curiosity and reverence.

"Banking institutions," Kato explains, "serve as the cornerstone of our financial system, providing essential services such as deposits, loans, and payment processing. Through their networks of branches and ATMs, they connect individuals, businesses, and governments, facilitating the flow of funds and fostering economic activity."

He gestures to the nearby bank building, its façade a

symbol of security and stability. "As custodians of our savings and investments, banks play a crucial role in financial intermediation—channeling funds from savers to borrowers, allocating capital to where it is most needed, and fueling investment and innovation."

Kato then turns his attention to the concept of financial intermediation. "In addition to providing a safe haven for deposits, banks act as intermediaries between savers and borrowers, matching surplus funds with investment opportunities. Whether it be financing a new business venture or funding a home purchase, banks bridge the gap between lenders and borrowers, facilitating economic growth and prosperity."

A young woman named Grace raises her hand. "But what about access to banking services? How can we ensure that everyone in our community has access to the financial tools they need to thrive?"

Kato's expression softens with empathy. "Ah, Grace, a question that strikes at the heart of financial inclusion. While access to banking services may be limited for some, there are initiatives we can undertake to expand access and empower individuals to participate fully in the economy."

He shares stories of community-based banking initiatives and microfinance programs that have transformed lives and lifted people out of poverty. "Take the Ndola Savings and Credit Cooperative, for example," Kato says, nodding to the cooperative members in the crowd. "Through collective action and mutual support, they have created a platform for financial empowerment, providing savings accounts, loans, and other services to their members."

The cooperative members nod in agreement, their faces

reflecting a sense of pride and solidarity.

Kato concludes with a call to action. "Let us embrace the power of community-based banking initiatives, advocate for policies that promote financial inclusion, and work together to build a future where everyone has access to the financial tools they need to thrive."

As the session draws to a close, the crowd is filled with a renewed sense of purpose and determination. With clarity in their minds and unity in their hearts, they disperse into the day, ready to apply their newfound understanding of banking institutions and financial intermediation to their everyday lives.

Kato watches them go, his heart swelling with pride. He knows that with trust as their foundation and solidarity as their strength, the residents of Ndola can build a future where prosperity knows no bounds.

Central Banking and Monetary Policy Tools

"Guiding the Currents of Prosperity: Central Banking and Monetary Policy in Ndola"

As the sun reaches its zenith over Ndola, casting a warm glow over the city, Kato returns to the community center, prepared to delve into the intricate workings of central banking and monetary policy. The air is filled with a sense of anticipation as the residents gather once more, eager to gain insights into the forces that shape their economic landscape.

Kato stands before the attentive crowd, his voice resonating with authority and clarity. "Good afternoon, my friends. Today, we journey deeper into the realm of finance, exploring

CHAPTER 4: MONEY, BANKING, AND MONETARY POLICY

the pivotal role of central banking and monetary policy in steering the currents of prosperity in our beloved Ndola. But fear not, for together, we shall navigate these waters with wisdom and understanding."

He begins with a reflective tone. "In the tapestry of our economy, central banking is the anchor of stability, the guardian of monetary policy, and the steward of prosperity. But let us not be overwhelmed by its complexity, for within the halls of the central bank lie the tools and mechanisms that shape our economic destiny."

The crowd listens intently, their faces reflecting a mix of curiosity and reverence.

"Central banking," Kato explains, "is entrusted with the responsibility of maintaining price stability, promoting full employment, and fostering sustainable economic growth. Through its monetary policy tools and interventions, the central bank seeks to balance the competing objectives of inflation control and economic expansion."

He gestures to the nearby branch of the central bank, its façade a symbol of authority and reliability. "As the custodian of our nation's monetary policy, the central bank employs a range of tools to achieve its objectives, including open market operations, reserve requirements, and interest rate adjustments."

Kato then turns his attention to the concept of open market operations. "In addition to setting interest rates, the central bank engages in open market operations—buying and selling government securities in the open market—to influence the money supply and interest rates. By adjusting the supply of money and credit in the economy, the central bank can affect borrowing costs, investment decisions, and ultimately, economic activity."

A middle-aged man named Joseph raises his hand. "But what about the impact of monetary policy on inflation and unemployment? How can the central bank strike a balance between these competing objectives?"

Kato's expression softens with empathy. "Ah, Joseph, an insightful question indeed. While the relationship between monetary policy, inflation, and unemployment is complex, the central bank strives to achieve both price stability and full employment through careful calibration of its policy instruments."

He shares stories of successful monetary policy interventions that have helped steer the economy through challenging times and fostered growth and stability. "Take the recent recession," Kato says, nodding to the audience. "Through decisive action and prudent policy adjustments, the central bank helped cushion the impact of the downturn and lay the foundation for recovery and renewal."

The audience nods in agreement, their faces reflecting a sense of appreciation for the central bank's role in safeguarding their economic well-being.

Kato concludes with a call to action. "Let us embrace the power of central banking and monetary policy as instruments of economic stability and prosperity. By understanding the tools and mechanisms at play, we can contribute to a future where every individual has the opportunity to thrive and succeed."

As the session draws to a close, the crowd is filled with a renewed sense of understanding and appreciation. With clarity in their minds and confidence in their hearts, they disperse into the afternoon, ready to apply their newfound knowledge of central banking and monetary policy to their everyday lives.

Kato watches them go, his heart swelling with pride. He knows that with knowledge as their compass and wisdom as their guide, the residents of Ndola can navigate the currents of prosperity and build a future where stability and growth go hand in hand.

The Role of Interest Rates in Economic Stability

"Balancing Acts: Unveiling the Role of Interest Rates in Economic Stability"

As the twilight descends upon Ndola, casting a gentle glow over the city, Kato returns to the community center, prepared to illuminate the intricate dance of interest rates in maintaining economic stability. The air is filled with anticipation as the residents gather once more, eager to uncover the mysteries of this essential component of financial management.

Kato stands before the attentive crowd, his voice resonating with authority and clarity. "Good evening, my friends. Today, we embark on a journey deeper into the realm of finance, exploring the pivotal role of interest rates in maintaining economic stability in our beloved Ndola. But fear not, for together, we shall unravel the complexities of this vital economic instrument."

He begins with a reflective tone. "In the fabric of our economy, interest rates are the threads that weave through every transaction, every investment, and every decision. But let us not be overwhelmed by their omnipresence, for within the dynamics of interest rates lie the mechanisms that govern our financial landscape."

The crowd listens intently, their faces reflecting a mix of curiosity and anticipation.

"Interest rates," Kato explains, "are not just numbers on a screen—they are signals of economic conditions, drivers of investment behavior, and instruments of monetary policy. Through their fluctuations, they influence borrowing costs, savings behavior, and ultimately, the trajectory of economic growth."

He gestures to the nearby bank buildings, their towering structures a testament to the power of finance. "As custodians of our nation's monetary policy, the central bank wields interest rates as a tool to achieve its objectives of price stability and full employment. By adjusting interest rates, the central bank can influence spending and investment decisions, thereby steering the economy towards its desired path."

Kato then turns his attention to the impact of interest rates on borrowing and lending. "In addition to its role in monetary policy, interest rates play a crucial role in the dynamics of borrowing and lending. When interest rates are low, borrowing becomes cheaper, stimulating investment and consumption. Conversely, when interest rates are high, borrowing becomes more expensive, dampening demand and curbing inflationary pressures."

A young entrepreneur named Sarah raises her hand. "But what about savers? How do changes in interest rates affect those who rely on interest income for their livelihood?"

Kato's expression softens with empathy. "Ah, Sarah, an important question indeed. While changes in interest rates may impact savers differently depending on their circumstances, the central bank aims to strike a balance between the needs of borrowers and savers in its monetary policy decisions."

He shares stories of individuals who have navigated the ups and downs of interest rates with resilience and adaptability. "Take John, for example," Kato says, nodding to the elderly gentleman in the crowd. "Despite fluctuations in interest rates over the years, he diversified his investment portfolio, ensuring a steady stream of income to support his retirement."

John smiles, his eyes shining with wisdom and experience.

Kato concludes with a call to action. "Let us embrace the power of interest rates as instruments of economic stability and growth. By understanding their dynamics and implications, we can make informed decisions, navigate financial challenges, and build a future of prosperity for ourselves and our community."

As the session draws to a close, the crowd is filled with a renewed sense of understanding and empowerment. With clarity in their minds and confidence in their hearts, they disperse into the night, ready to apply their newfound knowledge of interest rates to their everyday lives.

Kato watches them go, his heart swelling with pride. He knows that with knowledge as their compass and resilience as their guide, the residents of Ndola can navigate the complexities of finance and build a future where stability and prosperity go hand in hand.

Inflation and Deflation Dynamics

"Navigating the Tides: Understanding Inflation and Deflation Dynamics"

As dawn breaks over Ndola, casting a soft golden hue over the city, Kato returns to the community center, ready to shed light on the ebbs and flows of inflation and deflation. The air is filled with a sense of anticipation as the residents gather once more, eager to grasp the intricacies of these economic phenomena.

Kato stands before the attentive crowd, his voice steady and reassuring. "Good morning, my friends. Today, we delve deeper into the realm of finance, exploring the dynamic forces of inflation and deflation that shape our economic landscape. But fear not, for together, we shall navigate these tides with knowledge and understanding."

He begins with a contemplative tone. "In the tapestry of our economy, inflation and deflation are the currents that ripple through every transaction, every investment, and every decision. But let us not be overwhelmed by their complexity, for within the dynamics of these forces lie the keys to economic stability and prosperity."

The crowd listens intently, their faces reflecting a mix of curiosity and concern.

"Inflation," Kato explains, "is the rise in the general level of prices over time. It erodes the purchasing power of money, making goods and services more expensive and reducing the value of savings. While moderate inflation is a sign of a healthy, growing economy, high or hyperinflation can lead to instability and economic hardship."

He gestures to the nearby marketplace, where vendors adjust their prices to keep up with rising costs. "As prices rise, consumers may find their budgets stretched thin, leading to a decrease in purchasing power and a decline in living standards. Conversely, businesses may struggle to maintain profit margins, leading to layoffs and economic uncertainty."

Kato then turns his attention to deflation. "On the other hand, deflation is the decrease in the general level of prices over time. While deflation may seem like a boon to consumers, as their purchasing power increases, it can also signal underlying weaknesses in the economy, such as weak demand, stagnant wages, and falling investment."

A young mother named Alice raises her hand. "But how can we protect ourselves from the impact of inflation and deflation? What steps can we take to safeguard our financial well-being?"

Kato's expression softens with empathy. "Ah, Alice, an important question indeed. While we may not be able to control the forces of inflation and deflation, there are steps we can take to mitigate their impact on our lives."

He shares stories of individuals who have navigated the challenges of inflation and deflation with resilience and foresight. "Take Mary, for example," Kato says, nodding to the woman in the crowd. "During times of inflation, she diversified her investment portfolio to include assets that tend to perform well in inflationary environments, such as real estate and commodities. And during periods of deflation, she focused on preserving liquidity and maintaining a stable income stream."

Mary smiles, her eyes shining with gratitude.

Kato concludes with a call to action. "Let us embrace the power of knowledge and preparation as tools for navigating the tides of inflation and deflation. By understanding their dynamics and implications, we can make informed decisions, protect our financial well-being, and build a future of stability and prosperity for ourselves and our community."

As the session draws to a close, the crowd is filled with a renewed sense of empowerment and resolve. With clarity in their minds and determination in their hearts, they disperse into the day, ready to apply their newfound understanding of inflation and deflation to their everyday lives.

Kato watches them go, his heart swelling with pride. He knows that with knowledge as their compass and resilience as their guide, the residents of Ndola can navigate the currents of economic uncertainty and build a future where prosperity knows no bounds.

Financial Crises and Regulatory Responses

"Weathering the Storm: Navigating Financial Crises and Regulatory Responses"

As dusk settles over Ndola, casting shadows that dance across the cityscape, Kato returns to the community center, prepared to shed light on the tumultuous waters of financial crises and regulatory responses. The air is thick with anticipation as the residents gather once more, eager to understand the mechanisms that govern stability and resilience in times of economic turmoil.

Kato stands before the attentive crowd, his voice steady and resolute. "Good evening, my friends. Today, we embark on a journey into the heart of finance, exploring the turbulent seas of financial crises and the regulatory measures designed to navigate them. But fear not, for together, we shall weather the storm with knowledge and preparedness."

He begins with a solemn reflection. "In the tapestry of our economy, financial crises are the tempests that test our resilience, shaking the foundations of stability and prosperity. But let us not be daunted by their ferocity, for within the chaos lie the seeds of renewal and reform."

The crowd listens intently, their faces reflecting a mix of apprehension and determination.

"Financial crises," Kato explains, "can take many forms, from banking panics and asset bubbles to sovereign debt defaults and currency crises. Regardless of their origin, these crises have one thing in common: they threaten to undermine confidence in the financial system, disrupt economic activity, and jeopardize the well-being of individuals and communities."

He gestures to the nearby bank buildings, their sturdy facades a testament to the resilience of the financial system. "In response to financial crises, regulators and policymakers implement a range of measures to restore stability and safeguard the interests of depositors, investors, and taxpayers. These measures may include liquidity injections, capital injections, and regulatory reforms aimed at addressing the root causes of the crisis."

Kato then turns his attention to the importance of regulatory responses. "Regulatory responses play a crucial role in mitigating the impact of financial crises and preventing future crises from occurring. By enforcing prudential regulations, conducting stress tests, and promoting transparency and accountability in the financial sector, regulators can build a resilient and robust financial system that is better equipped to withstand shocks and disruptions."

A concerned citizen named David raises his hand. "But what

can we, as individuals, do to protect ourselves from the fallout of financial crises? How can we prepare for the unexpected?"

Kato's expression softens with empathy. "Ah, David, an important question indeed. While we may not be able to predict the timing or severity of financial crises, there are steps we can take to safeguard our financial well-being."

He shares stories of individuals who have navigated financial crises with resilience and foresight. "Take Samuel, for example," Kato says, nodding to the man in the crowd. "During the last financial crisis, he maintained a diversified investment portfolio, ensuring that his assets were spread across different asset classes and geographic regions. He also maintained an emergency fund to cover unexpected expenses and relied on sound financial advice to navigate the turbulent waters."

Samuel nods in agreement, his face a picture of determination.

Kato concludes with a call to action. "Let us embrace the power of preparedness and vigilance as tools for navigating financial crises. By understanding the warning signs, taking prudent precautions, and staying informed about regulatory developments, we can protect our financial well-being and build a future of resilience and prosperity for ourselves and our community."

As the session draws to a close, the crowd is filled with a renewed sense of empowerment and resolve. With knowledge as their shield and preparedness as their armor, they disperse into the night, ready to face whatever challenges the future may hold.

Kato watches them go, his heart swelling with pride. He knows that with vigilance as their guide and solidarity as their strength, the residents of Ndola can weather any storm and emerge stronger on the other side.

5

Chapter 5: Economic Growth and Development

Theories of Economic Growth

"Seeds of Progress: Cultivating Economic Growth and Development"

In the heart of Ndola, where the rhythm of life pulses through the bustling streets, Kato returns to the community center, prepared to sow the seeds of economic growth and development. The air is charged with anticipation as the residents gather once more, eager to explore the theories that underpin the path to prosperity.

Kato stands before the assembled crowd, his presence a beacon of hope amidst the sea of eager faces. "Good morning, my friends. Today, we embark on a journey to explore the theories of economic growth—the driving forces behind the transformation of nations and the improvement of livelihoods. But fear not, for together, we shall cultivate a

CHAPTER 5: ECONOMIC GROWTH AND DEVELOPMENT

deeper understanding of the pathways to progress."

He begins with a contemplative reflection. "In the tapestry of our society, economic growth is the fruit of innovation, investment, and hard work—a testament to human ingenuity and perseverance. But let us not be blinded by its allure, for within the theories of economic growth lie the keys to unlocking our collective potential."

The crowd listens intently, their expressions a mix of curiosity and anticipation.

"Economic growth," Kato explains, "is the increase in the production of goods and services over time—an engine of prosperity that raises living standards, creates opportunities, and fosters progress. But what drives this growth? What are the theories that explain the mechanisms behind this phenomenon?"

He gestures to the nearby fields, where farmers toil under the sun to cultivate their crops. "Theories of economic growth posit various factors that contribute to the expansion of an economy, from increases in physical capital and labor productivity to technological innovation and institutional reforms."

Kato then turns his attention to the concept of capital accumulation. "One theory of economic growth emphasizes the importance of capital accumulation— the process of increasing the stock of physical and human capital through investment in infrastructure, education, and technology. By investing in capital goods and improving human capital through education and training, countries can enhance their productivity and spur economic growth."

A young entrepreneur named Chanda raises her hand. "But what about innovation? How does technological progress drive economic growth and development?"

Kato's expression softens with empathy. "Ah, Chanda, an astute question indeed. Another theory of economic growth highlights the role of technological innovation as a catalyst for economic progress. Through research and development, technological advances, and the diffusion of knowledge, countries can unleash the forces of innovation and drive long-term economic growth."

He shares stories of nations that have embraced innovation and technological progress to propel their economies forward. "Take Singapore, for example," Kato says, nodding to the city-state's achievements. "Through strategic investments in education, research, and technology, Singapore has transformed itself from a resource-poor island nation into a global hub of innovation and entrepreneurship."

The audience nods in agreement, their faces reflecting a sense of admiration and inspiration.

Kato concludes with a call to action. "Let us embrace the power of innovation and investment as engines of economic growth and development. By understanding the theories that underpin progress, we can chart a course towards a future where prosperity knows no bounds."

As the session draws to a close, the crowd is filled with a renewed sense of purpose and determination. With knowledge as their compass and innovation as their guiding star, they disperse into the day, ready to sow the seeds of progress and cultivate a future of prosperity for themselves and their community.

Kato watches them go, his heart swelling with pride. He knows that with determination as their fuel and ingenuity as their plow, the residents of Ndola can cultivate a future where economic growth and development flourish like fields in full bloom.

Factors Influencing Economic Development

"Pillars of Progress: Unraveling Factors Influencing Economic Development"

As the sun reaches its zenith over Ndola, casting a warm glow over the city, Kato returns to the community center, ready to delve deeper into the factors that shape economic development. The air is filled with a sense of anticipation as the residents gather once more, eager to unravel the mysteries of progress and prosperity.

Kato stands before the assembled crowd, his voice a beacon of clarity amidst the sea of curious faces. "Good afternoon, my friends. Today, we continue our journey into the realm of economic development, exploring the factors that influence the path to prosperity. But fear not, for together, we shall uncover the pillars of progress."

He begins with a reflective tone. "In the tapestry of our society, economic development is the culmination of various factors—geographical, social, political, and economic—that shape the destiny of nations and communities. But let us not be overwhelmed by their complexity, for within these factors lie the keys to unlocking our potential and building a brighter future."

The crowd listens intently, their faces reflecting a mix of curiosity and determination.

"Geographical factors," Kato explains, "play a significant role in determining the economic fortunes of a region. Access to natural resources, proximity to markets, and the presence of navigable waterways can all influence the pace and trajectory of economic development. For example, regions blessed with abundant natural resources may have a comparative advantage in industries such as mining, agriculture, or tourism, which can drive economic growth and prosperity."

He gestures to the nearby landscape, where the rich soil yields bountiful harvests and the rivers flow with life-giving waters. "In Ndola, our natural resources—such as copper, agriculture, and tourism—have long been pillars of our economy, providing employment opportunities and fueling economic activity."

Kato then turns his attention to social and political factors. "Social and political stability are essential prerequisites for economic development. A peaceful and inclusive society, characterized by respect for human rights, rule of law, and political stability, provides a conducive environment for investment, entrepreneurship, and innovation. Conversely, social unrest, corruption, and political instability can deter investors, hinder economic growth, and perpetuate poverty."

A concerned citizen named Esther raises her hand. "But what about education and human capital development? How do they contribute to economic development and prosperity?"

Kato's expression softens with empathy. "Ah, Esther, an important question indeed. Education and human capital development are fundamental drivers of economic development, empowering individuals with the knowledge, skills, and capabilities to participate fully in the economy, adapt to changing circumstances, and drive innovation and productivity growth."

He shares stories of communities that have invested in

education and human capital development to transform their economies and improve livelihoods. "Take the Nordic countries, for example," Kato says, nodding to their achievements. "Through robust education systems, lifelong learning opportunities, and investments in health care and social services, they have built prosperous and inclusive societies where human capital is the engine of economic growth."

The audience nods in agreement, their faces reflecting a sense of admiration and determination.

Kato concludes with a call to action. "Let us embrace the power of geography, social cohesion, and human capital development as pillars of economic development and prosperity. By understanding the factors that influence our economic destiny, we can chart a course towards a future where every individual has the opportunity to thrive and succeed."

As the session draws to a close, the crowd is filled with a renewed sense of understanding and resolve. With clarity in their minds and unity in their hearts, they disperse into the afternoon, ready to apply their newfound knowledge to their everyday lives.

Kato watches them go, his heart swelling with pride. He knows that with determination as their compass and solidarity as their strength, the residents of Ndola can chart a course towards a future where economic development and prosperity flourish for all.

Human Development Index and Quality of Life Indicators

"Beyond Numbers: Nurturing Human Development and Quality of Life"

As the twilight descends over Ndola, casting a soft glow over the city, Kato returns to the community center, prepared to delve deeper into the essence of human development and quality of life. The air is filled with a sense of contemplation as the residents gather once more, eager to explore the intricacies of progress beyond mere economic measures.

Kato stands before the assembled crowd, his voice carrying a sense of reverence for the topic at hand. "Good evening, my friends. Today, we journey into the realm of human development and quality of life, exploring the nuances of progress that extend beyond economic indicators. But fear not, for together, we shall uncover the true measure of prosperity—the well-being and dignity of every individual."

He begins with a reflective tone. "In the fabric of our society, human development is the truest measure of progress—a reflection of our collective efforts to nurture the potential and dignity of every individual. But let us not be blinded by the allure of material wealth, for within the Human Development Index and quality of life indicators lie the essence of our shared humanity."

The crowd listens intently, their faces reflecting a mix of introspection and anticipation.

"The Human Development Index (HDI)," Kato explains, "is a composite measure that captures three dimensions of human development: health, education, and standard of living. By considering factors such as life expectancy, educational attainment, and income per capita, the HDI provides a more holistic view of progress that extends beyond GDP and economic growth."

He gestures to the nearby health clinic, where doctors and nurses work tirelessly to care for the sick and vulnerable. "Health is a fundamental component of human development, enabling individuals to lead fulfilling and productive lives. Access to healthcare services, clean water, sanitation, and nutritious food are essential determinants of health outcomes and quality of life."

Kato then turns his attention to education. "Education is the cornerstone of human development, empowering individuals with the knowledge, skills, and capabilities to realize their full potential and contribute meaningfully to society. Access to quality education, lifelong learning opportunities, and gender equality in education are critical drivers of progress and prosperity."

A young mother named Fatima raises her hand. "But what about the standard of living? How can we ensure that every individual has the opportunity to enjoy a decent standard of living and a life of dignity?"

Kato's expression softens with empathy. "Ah, Fatima, an important question indeed. The standard of living encompasses various factors, including income, housing, employment, and social protection. Ensuring access to decent work, affordable housing, social safety nets, and inclusive economic opportunities are essential for improving living standards and promoting human development."

He shares stories of communities that have embraced human development and quality of life as guiding principles for progress. "Take Bhutan, for example," Kato says, nodding to the country's achievements. "Through its Gross National Happiness Index, Bhutan has prioritized holistic well-being over mere economic growth, fostering a society where happiness and harmony are valued as much as material wealth."

The audience nods in agreement, their faces reflecting a sense of resonance and inspiration.

Kato concludes with a call to action. "Let us embrace the Human Development Index and quality of life indicators as measures of progress that honor the dignity and well-being of every individual. By investing in health, education, and standard of living, we can build a future where prosperity is measured not just in dollars and cents, but in the richness of human experience and the depth of human connection."

As the session draws to a close, the crowd is filled with a renewed sense of purpose and determination. With compassion in their hearts and solidarity in their actions, they disperse into the night, ready to nurture human development and quality of life for themselves and their community.

Kato watches them go, his heart swelling with pride. He knows that with empathy as their compass and resilience as their guide, the residents of Ndola can build a future where prosperity is not just a distant dream, but a tangible reality for all.

Global Economic Disparities and Inequality

CHAPTER 5: ECONOMIC GROWTH AND DEVELOPMENT

"Bridging Divides: Confronting Global Economic Disparities and Inequality"

As dawn breaks over Ndola, illuminating the city with a golden glow, Kato returns to the community center, ready to confront the stark realities of global economic disparities and inequality. The air is charged with a sense of urgency as the residents gather once more, eager to address the systemic challenges that divide nations and communities.

Kato stands before the assembled crowd, his voice resonating with determination. "Good morning, my friends. Today, we confront the formidable challenges of global economic disparities and inequality—forces that threaten to undermine the fabric of our society and perpetuate injustice. But fear not, for together, we shall shine a light on these disparities and work towards a future of equity and justice for all."

He begins with a somber reflection. "In the mosaic of our world, economic disparities and inequality are the shadows that darken the promise of progress, dividing nations and communities along lines of wealth, opportunity, and privilege. But let us not be resigned to their presence, for within our collective efforts lie the power to bridge these divides and build a more just and inclusive world."

The crowd listens intently, their faces reflecting a mix of concern and determination.

"Global economic disparities," Kato explains, "are the result of uneven development, unequal distribution of resources, and systemic barriers that hinder access to opportunities and basic necessities. While some regions enjoy prosperity and abundance, others languish in poverty and deprivation, trapped in cycles of inequality and marginalization."

He gestures to the nearby map of the world, where regions marked by affluence stand in stark contrast to those marked by poverty and underdevelopment. "In Ndola, we are not immune to the impacts of global economic disparities. Despite our rich natural resources and resilient spirit, we are acutely aware of the challenges that persist in our own community and beyond."

Kato then turns his attention to the root causes of inequality. "At the heart of global economic disparities lie systemic injustices—such as unequal access to education, healthcare, and economic opportunities—that perpetuate cycles of poverty and marginalization. Structural barriers, discriminatory policies, and power imbalances further exacerbate inequality, widening the gap between the haves and the have-nots."

A concerned citizen named Joseph raises his hand. "But what can we do to address these disparities? How can we work towards a more equitable and just world?"

Kato's expression softens with empathy. "Ah, Joseph, an important question indeed. Addressing global economic disparities and inequality requires a multi-faceted approach that combines policy reforms, social investments, and collective action."

He shares stories of individuals and communities that have taken bold steps to confront inequality and injustice, from grassroots movements advocating for social justice to international efforts to promote fair trade and economic empowerment.

"By advocating for policy reforms that promote inclusive growth, investing in education and healthcare, and challenging systems of oppression and exploitation, we can build a future where every individual has the opportunity to thrive and succeed," Kato says, nodding to the crowd.

The audience nods in agreement, their faces reflecting a sense of solidarity and determination.

Kato concludes with a call to action. "Let us stand together as champions of equity and justice, committed to building a world where economic disparities and inequality are relics of the past. By recognizing our shared humanity and working towards a common purpose, we can bridge divides and create a future where prosperity is truly inclusive and sustainable for all."

As the session draws to a close, the crowd is filled with a renewed sense of purpose and solidarity. With determination in their hearts and solidarity in their actions, they disperse into the day, ready to confront global economic disparities and inequality with courage and conviction.

Kato watches them go, his heart swelling with pride. He knows that with unity as their strength and justice as their guide, the residents of Ndola can pave the way towards a future where prosperity knows no boundaries and every individual is afforded dignity and respect.

Sustainable Development Goals and Environmental Economics

"Harmony in Progress: Pursuing Sustainable Development Goals and Environmental Economics"

As the sun sets over Ndola, painting the sky in hues of pink and orange, Kato returns to the community center, ready to explore the pathways to sustainable development and environmental stewardship. The air is filled with a sense of purpose as the residents gather once more, eager to embrace a future where prosperity is balanced with environmental responsibility.

Kato stands before the assembled crowd, his voice carrying the weight of urgency and hope. "Good evening, my friends. Today, we embark on a journey towards sustainable development—a path that seeks to harmonize economic prosperity with environmental preservation. But fear not, for together, we shall pave the way towards a future where progress is measured not just in wealth, but in the health of our planet and the well-being of future generations."

He begins with a solemn reflection. "In the tapestry of our world, sustainable development is the promise of a brighter future—a future where economic growth is not pursued at the expense of our planet, but in harmony with nature. But let us not underestimate the challenges that lie ahead, for achieving sustainable development requires bold action, collective effort, and unwavering commitment."

The crowd listens intently, their faces reflecting a mix of determination and concern.

"Sustainable Development Goals (SDGs)," Kato explains, "are a set of universal goals adopted by the United Nations to address the most pressing social, economic, and environmental challenges facing humanity. From ending poverty and hunger to promoting clean energy and climate action, the SDGs provide a roadmap for building a more just, equitable, and sustainable world."

He gestures to the nearby park, where children play amidst the trees and flowers. "In Ndola, we are committed to advancing the SDGs and promoting environmental sustainability. From sustainable agriculture and renewable energy to conservation efforts and waste management, we recognize the importance of preserving our natural resources and protecting the planet for future generations."

Kato then turns his attention to the field of environmental economics. "Environmental economics," he explains, "is a branch of economics that seeks to understand the relationship between economic activity and the environment, and to develop policies and solutions that promote sustainable development and environmental conservation. By incorporating the value of natural resources and ecosystem services into decision-making processes, environmental economics aims to reconcile economic growth with environmental protection."

A concerned environmentalist named Aisha raises her hand. "But what can we do to address the environmental challenges facing our community? How can we work towards a future where economic development is sustainable and environmentally responsible?"

Kato's expression softens with empathy. "Ah, Aisha, an important question indeed. Addressing environmental challenges requires a multi-faceted approach that combines policy reforms, technological innovations, and individual actions."

He shares stories of communities that have embraced sustainable practices and environmental stewardship to protect the planet and promote prosperity. "Take Costa Rica, for example," Kato says, nodding to the country's achievements. "Through its commitment to conservation, renewable energy, and ecotourism, Costa Rica has become a global leader in sustainable development, demonstrating that economic growth and environmental protection can go hand in hand."

The audience nods in agreement, their faces reflecting a sense of inspiration and determination.

Kato concludes with a call to action. "Let us embrace the Sustainable Development Goals and environmental economics as guiding principles for progress, committed to building a future where prosperity is sustainable, equitable, and inclusive for all. By working together, we can protect our planet, promote economic growth, and create a legacy of stewardship for future generations."

As the session draws to a close, the crowd is filled with a renewed sense of purpose and resolve. With determination in their hearts and unity in their actions, they disperse into the night, ready to embrace the challenge of sustainable development and environmental stewardship.

Kato watches them go, his heart swelling with pride. He knows that with commitment as their compass and sustainability as their guide, the residents of Ndola can pave the way towards a future where prosperity and environmental preservation go hand in hand, ensuring a legacy of harmony and abundance for generations to come.

Strategies for Promoting Inclusive Growth

CHAPTER 5: ECONOMIC GROWTH AND DEVELOPMENT

"Unity in Progress: Fostering Inclusive Growth Strategies"

As the city of Ndola awakens to a new day, vibrant with the promise of possibility, Kato returns to the community center, ready to unveil strategies for fostering inclusive growth. The air is charged with anticipation as the residents gather once more, eager to explore pathways that ensure prosperity reaches every corner of their community.

Kato stands before the assembled crowd, his voice resonating with determination and hope. "Good morning, my friends. Today, we embark on a journey towards inclusive growth—a path that seeks to empower every individual, regardless of their background or circumstances, to participate in and benefit from the fruits of progress. But fear not, for together, we shall forge a future where no one is left behind."

He begins with a resolute reflection. "In the tapestry of our society, inclusive growth is the promise of a brighter tomorrow—a future where prosperity is not a privilege reserved for the few, but a right shared by all. But let us not be complacent in our aspirations, for achieving inclusive growth requires bold action, visionary leadership, and unwavering commitment."

The crowd listens intently, their faces reflecting a mix of determination and hope.

"Inclusive growth," Kato explains, "is characterized by equitable opportunities, shared benefits, and broad-based participation in the economy. It goes beyond mere economic growth to ensure that the benefits of development are distributed fairly and that every individual has the opportunity to fulfill their potential and contribute to society."

He gestures to the diverse faces in the audience, representing different backgrounds and experiences. "In Ndola, we recognize the importance of promoting inclusive growth and creating opportunities for all members of our community. From investing in education and skills development to supporting small businesses and entrepreneurship, we are committed to building an inclusive economy where everyone can thrive."

Kato then turns his attention to the importance of social protection and safety nets. "Social protection programs, such as cash transfers, food assistance, and healthcare subsidies, play a crucial role in promoting inclusive growth by providing a safety net for the most vulnerable members of society. By ensuring access to basic necessities and social services, we can reduce poverty, inequality, and social exclusion, fostering a more equitable and inclusive society."

A concerned community leader named David raises his hand. "But what can we do to ensure that our efforts towards inclusive growth are sustainable and lasting? How can we build a future where prosperity is truly shared by all?"

Kato's expression softens with empathy. "Ah, David, an important question indeed. Building a future of inclusive growth requires a comprehensive approach that addresses the root causes of inequality and fosters economic empowerment for all."

He shares stories of communities that have embraced inclusive growth strategies to uplift marginalized groups and promote social cohesion. "Take Rwanda, for example," Kato says, nodding to the country's achievements. "Through its Vision 2020 initiative, Rwanda has prioritized inclusive growth and poverty reduction, investing in education, healthcare, and infrastructure to create opportunities for all citizens, regardless of their background or circumstances."

The audience nods in agreement, their faces reflecting a sense of determination and solidarity.

Kato concludes with a call to action. "Let us embrace inclusive growth as a guiding principle for progress, committed to building a future where prosperity is shared by all members of our community. By investing in education, social protection, and economic empowerment, we can create a society where every individual has the opportunity to thrive and succeed."

As the session draws to a close, the crowd is filled with a renewed sense of purpose and resolve. With determination in their hearts and unity in their actions, they disperse into the day, ready to embrace the challenge of promoting inclusive growth and building a future where prosperity knows no boundaries.

Kato watches them go, his heart swelling with pride. He knows that with commitment as their compass and inclusivity as their guide, the residents of Ndola can pave the way towards a future where prosperity is not just a distant dream, but a tangible reality for all.

6

Chapter 6: International Trade and Finance

Theories of Comparative Advantage

"Bridging Borders: Exploring Theories of Comparative Advantage"

As the sun rises over Ndola, casting its golden rays upon the city, Kato returns to the community center, ready to unravel the mysteries of international trade and finance. The air is filled with a sense of curiosity and anticipation as the residents gather once more, eager to embark on a journey into the world of economic exchange and global connectivity.

Kato stands before the assembled crowd, his voice resonating with energy and enthusiasm. "Good morning, my friends. Today, we delve into the realm of international trade and finance, exploring the theories that underpin the exchange of goods, services, and capital across borders. But fear not, for together, we shall unravel the complexities of global economics and discover the pathways to prosperity."

He begins with a contemplative reflection. "In the tapestry of our interconnected world, international trade is the thread that binds nations together, fostering cooperation, competition, and mutual benefit. But let us not be daunted by its vastness, for within the theories of comparative advantage lie the keys to unlocking the potential of nations and maximizing global welfare."

The crowd listens intently, their faces reflecting a mix of curiosity and intrigue.

"Comparative advantage," Kato explains, "is a fundamental principle in economics that states that countries should specialize in the production of goods and services in which they have a lower opportunity cost, and trade with other nations to obtain goods and services in which they have a higher opportunity cost. By specializing in the production of goods and services in which they are relatively more efficient, countries can increase their overall output and consumption, leading to greater prosperity for all."

He gestures to the nearby marketplace, where vendors display goods from far-off lands, showcasing the diversity and abundance of global trade. "In Ndola, we are no strangers to the benefits of international trade. From the copper mines that fuel our economy to the agricultural products that nourish our communities, we rely on trade to meet our needs and enhance our standard of living."

Kato then turns his attention to the theories that underpin comparative advantage. "Classical economists, such as David Ricardo, first articulated the theory of comparative advantage in the early 19th century. Ricardo argued that even if one country is more efficient than another country in producing all goods, both countries can still benefit from trade if they specialize in producing the goods in which they have a comparative advantage and trade with each other."

A curious student named Mary raises her hand. "But how do countries determine their comparative advantage? What factors influence their specialization and trade patterns?"

Kato's expression softens with empathy. "Ah, Mary, an astute question indeed. Comparative advantage is determined by a combination of factors, including natural resources, technological capabilities, labor skills, and capital endowments. Countries often specialize in the production of goods and services that make the most efficient use of their resources and capabilities, taking into account factors such as climate, geography, and historical patterns of trade."

He shares stories of nations that have leveraged their comparative advantages to achieve economic success and prosperity. "Take Japan, for example," Kato says, nodding to the country's achievements. "Despite its limited natural resources, Japan has become a global leader in technology and manufacturing by investing in education, research, and innovation, and leveraging its skilled workforce and strong work ethic to compete in the global marketplace."

The audience nods in agreement, their faces reflecting a sense of understanding and appreciation.

Kato concludes with a call to action. "Let us embrace the principles of comparative advantage as guiding principles for international trade, committed to fostering cooperation, competition, and mutual benefit among nations. By understanding our strengths and leveraging our capabilities, we can build a future where prosperity knows no borders and every nation has the opportunity to thrive and succeed."

As the session draws to a close, the crowd is filled with a renewed sense of curiosity and enlightenment. With knowledge as their compass and cooperation as their guide, they disperse into the day, ready to explore the world of international trade and finance with newfound insight and understanding.

Kato watches them go, his heart swelling with pride. He knows that with curiosity as their fuel and cooperation as their currency, the residents of Ndola can navigate the complexities of global economics and build a future of prosperity and abundance for all.

Trade Policies and Tariffs

"Navigating Boundaries: Understanding Trade Policies and Tariffs"

As the day progresses in Ndola, Kato returns to the community center, ready to delve deeper into the intricacies of international trade. The air hums with anticipation as the residents gather once more, eager to unravel the complexities of trade policies and tariffs that shape the flow of goods and capital across borders.

Kato stands before the assembled crowd, his voice projecting a sense of authority and conviction. "Good afternoon, my friends. Today, we continue our exploration of international trade, focusing on the policies and tariffs that influence the movement of goods and services between nations. But fear not, for together, we shall navigate the boundaries of global commerce and uncover the strategies that nations employ to protect their interests."

He begins with a contemplative reflection. "In the mosaic of global economics, trade policies and tariffs are the tools that nations wield to safeguard their industries, promote domestic production, and regulate the flow of goods and services. But let us not be blinded by their complexity, for within these policies lie the potential to shape the destiny of nations and communities."

The crowd listens intently, their faces reflecting a mix of curiosity and concern.

"Trade policies," Kato explains, "are government actions and regulations that influence the flow of goods and services between countries. These policies can take various forms, including tariffs, quotas, subsidies, and trade agreements, and are often designed to protect domestic industries, promote exports, and address trade imbalances."

He gestures to the nearby factory, where workers labor tirelessly to produce goods for export. "In Ndola, we rely on trade policies to protect our industries and promote economic growth. From tariffs on imported goods to export subsidies for local producers, these policies play a crucial role in shaping our economy and ensuring our competitiveness in the global marketplace."

Kato then turns his attention to tariffs. "Tariffs," he explains, "are taxes or duties imposed on imported goods, making them more expensive for consumers and businesses. Tariffs can be used to protect domestic industries from foreign competition, generate revenue for the government, and address trade imbalances. However, they can also lead to higher prices for consumers, reduce consumer choice, and distort international trade patterns."

A concerned business owner named Joseph raises his hand. "But how do tariffs affect businesses and consumers? Are there any strategies for navigating the challenges posed by tariffs?"

Kato's expression softens with empathy. "Ah, Joseph, an important question indeed. Tariffs can have significant implications for businesses, consumers, and the economy as a whole. For businesses, tariffs can increase the cost of imported inputs and raw materials, reduce competitiveness in foreign markets, and disrupt global supply chains. For consumers, tariffs can lead to higher prices for imported goods, reducing purchasing power and limiting consumer choice."

He shares stories of businesses that have navigated the challenges of tariffs by diversifying their supply chains, investing in domestic production, and advocating for trade policies that promote fair competition and open markets. "By understanding the impact of tariffs and adapting to changing trade dynamics, businesses can mitigate risks, seize opportunities, and thrive in the global marketplace," Kato says, nodding to the crowd.

The audience nods in agreement, their faces reflecting a sense of determination and resilience.

Kato concludes with a call to action. "Let us embrace trade policies and tariffs as tools for shaping the future of our economy, committed to fostering a balanced and equitable global trading system that benefits all nations and communities. By working together and advocating for policies that promote openness, fairness, and sustainability, we can build a future where prosperity knows no boundaries and every individual has the opportunity to thrive and succeed."

As the session draws to a close, the crowd is filled with a

renewed sense of understanding and resolve. With knowledge as their compass and collaboration as their guide, they disperse into the afternoon, ready to navigate the complexities of global commerce with confidence and determination.

Kato watches them go, his heart swelling with pride. He knows that with resilience as their currency and unity as their strength, the residents of Ndola can overcome the challenges of trade policies and tariffs and build a future of prosperity and abundance for all.

Exchange Rates and Foreign Exchange Markets

"Currency of Connections: Exploring Exchange Rates and Foreign Exchange Markets"

As the evening descends upon Ndola, Kato returns to the community center, ready to unravel the mysteries of exchange rates and foreign exchange markets. The atmosphere is charged with curiosity and intrigue as the residents gather once more, eager to understand the forces that shape the value of currencies and drive the global flow of capital.

Kato stands before the assembled crowd, his voice resonating with clarity and authority. "Good evening, my friends. Today, we embark on a journey into the world of exchange rates and foreign exchange markets—a realm where currencies rise and fall, and fortunes are made and lost. But fear not, for together, we shall demystify these concepts and uncover the mechanisms that govern global finance."

He begins with a reflective tone. "In the tapestry of international trade and finance, exchange rates are the threads that connect nations, facilitating the exchange of goods, services,

CHAPTER 6: INTERNATIONAL TRADE AND FINANCE

and capital across borders. But let us not be intimidated by their complexity, for within the fluctuations of exchange rates lie the pulse of the global economy and the heartbeat of nations."

The crowd listens intently, their faces reflecting a mix of fascination and apprehension.

"Exchange rates," Kato explains, "are the prices at which one currency can be exchanged for another currency. They are determined by supply and demand in the foreign exchange market, where buyers and sellers come together to trade currencies and conduct transactions. Exchange rates play a crucial role in shaping international trade, investment, and monetary policy, influencing the competitiveness of nations and the stability of financial markets."

He gestures to the nearby marketplace, where traders exchange currencies amidst a flurry of activity. "In Ndola, we are no strangers to the impact of exchange rates on our economy. From importers purchasing goods from overseas to exporters selling products to foreign markets, exchange rates influence the cost of goods, the profitability of businesses, and the purchasing power of consumers."

Kato then turns his attention to the dynamics of foreign exchange markets. "Foreign exchange markets," he explains, "are decentralized markets where currencies are bought and sold, allowing participants to hedge against currency risk, speculate on exchange rate movements, and facilitate international trade and investment. These markets operate 24 hours a day, five days a week, across different time zones and continents, reflecting the global nature of finance and commerce."

A curious entrepreneur named Sarah raises her hand. "But

how do changes in exchange rates affect businesses and individuals? Are there any strategies for managing currency risk and navigating the complexities of foreign exchange markets?"

Kato's expression softens with empathy. "Ah, Sarah, an insightful question indeed. Changes in exchange rates can have significant implications for businesses, investors, and consumers. For businesses engaged in international trade, fluctuations in exchange rates can impact the cost of imported goods, the profitability of exports, and the value of foreign investments. For individuals, changes in exchange rates can affect the cost of travel, remittances, and foreign purchases."

He shares stories of businesses that have managed currency risk by hedging their exposure through financial instruments such as forward contracts, options, and currency swaps. "By understanding the dynamics of foreign exchange markets and implementing sound risk management strategies, businesses and individuals can mitigate the impact of exchange rate fluctuations and protect themselves against financial volatility," Kato says, nodding to the crowd.

The audience nods in agreement, their faces reflecting a sense of understanding and determination.

Kato concludes with a call to action. "Let us embrace the complexities of exchange rates and foreign exchange markets as opportunities for growth and innovation, committed to navigating the challenges of global finance with resilience and foresight. By staying informed, adopting best practices, and collaborating with others, we can build a future where the currency of connections bridges divides and fosters prosperity for all."

As the session draws to a close, the crowd is filled with a

renewed sense of confidence and empowerment. With knowledge as their compass and adaptability as their guide, they disperse into the night, ready to navigate the complexities of exchange rates and foreign exchange markets with newfound insight and understanding.

Kato watches them go, his heart swelling with pride. He knows that with determination as their currency and collaboration as their strength, the residents of Ndola can harness the power of global finance to build a future of prosperity and abundance for themselves and their community.

Balance of Payments and Current Account Imbalances

"Harmony in Transactions: Unraveling Balance of Payments and Current Account Imbalances"

As night falls over Ndola, Kato returns to the community center, ready to explore the intricacies of balance of payments and current account imbalances. The atmosphere is charged with anticipation as the residents gather once more, eager to understand the mechanisms that govern the flow of international transactions and shape the economic landscape.

Kato stands before the assembled crowd, his voice carrying a sense of purpose and clarity. "Good evening, my friends. Today, we delve deeper into the realm of global finance, focusing on the balance of payments and the implications of current account imbalances. But fear not, for together, we shall unravel the complexities of international transactions and uncover the pathways to economic stability and prosperity."

He begins with a reflective tone. "In the tapestry of international finance, the balance of payments is the ledger that records a nation's economic transactions with the rest of the world, encompassing trade in goods and services, financial flows, and transfers of assets. But let us not be intimidated by its complexity, for within the balance of payments lie the insights into a nation's economic health and its position in the global economy."

The crowd listens intently, their faces reflecting a mix of curiosity and concern.

"The balance of payments," Kato explains, "is divided into three main components: the current account, the capital account, and the financial account. The current account tracks the flow of goods and services, income, and transfers between a country and the rest of the world, while the capital account records capital transfers and the acquisition and disposal of non-financial assets. The financial account measures changes in ownership of financial assets and liabilities between residents and non-residents."

He gestures to the nearby trade routes, where goods and services crisscross borders in a complex dance of commerce. "In Ndola, we are connected to the global economy through our participation in trade and investment. The balance of payments reflects our transactions with other nations, capturing the exports we sell, the imports we purchase, the income we earn from abroad, and the aid and remittances we receive."

Kato then turns his attention to current account imbalances. "Current account imbalances," he explains, "occur when a country's imports exceed its exports, leading to a trade deficit, or when its exports surpass its imports, resulting in a trade surplus. These imbalances can have significant implications for a nation's economy, affecting its competitiveness, exchange rates, and overall economic stability."

A concerned economist named James raises his hand. "But how do current account imbalances impact a nation's economy? Are there any strategies for addressing these imbalances and promoting economic stability?"

Kato's expression softens with empathy. "Ah, James, an insightful question indeed. Current account imbalances can have various effects on a nation's economy, depending on the underlying causes and the policy responses adopted. Trade deficits, for example, can lead to a decline in the country's currency value, an increase in borrowing from abroad, and a loss of competitiveness in international markets. Trade surpluses, on the other hand, can lead to a stronger currency, increased savings, and potential trade tensions with trading partners."

He shares stories of countries that have addressed current account imbalances through a combination of policy measures, including fiscal and monetary policy adjustments, structural reforms, and exchange rate interventions. "By implementing sound economic policies and fostering a conducive business environment, countries can promote exports, reduce imports, and achieve a more balanced current account position," Kato says, nodding to the crowd.

The audience nods in agreement, their faces reflecting a sense of understanding and determination.

Kato concludes with a call to action. "Let us embrace the balance of payments as a window into our nation's economic health and a roadmap for policy action, committed to fostering economic stability and prosperity for all. By understanding the dynamics of international transactions and addressing current account imbalances, we can build a future where our economy thrives, our communities prosper, and our connections with the world grow stronger."

As the session draws to a close, the crowd is filled with a renewed sense of insight and resolve. With knowledge as their compass and collaboration as their guide, they disperse into the night, ready to navigate the complexities of global finance with confidence and determination.

Kato watches them go, his heart swelling with pride. He knows that with understanding as their currency and unity as their strength, the residents of Ndola can navigate the challenges of balance of payments and current account imbalances and build a future of prosperity and abundance for themselves and their community.

Trade Agreements and Regional Integration

"Bridging Borders: Embracing Trade Agreements and Regional Integration"

As dawn breaks over Ndola, Kato returns to the community center, ready to explore the transformative power of trade agreements and regional integration. The atmosphere is filled with anticipation as the residents gather once more, eager to understand how cooperation across borders can shape the economic landscape and foster prosperity for all.

Kato stands before the assembled crowd, his voice filled with conviction and optimism. "Good morning, my friends. Today, we embark on a journey into the world of trade agreements and regional integration—a realm where nations come together to forge partnerships, deepen economic ties, and unlock the potential of collective action. But fear not, for together, we shall explore the pathways to economic growth and prosperity through cooperation and collaboration."

He begins with a reflective tone. "In the tapestry of international relations, trade agreements and regional integration are the threads that weave together nations, creating a fabric of shared interests, mutual benefits, and common goals. But let us not be daunted by the challenges of cooperation, for within these agreements lie the opportunities to harness the strengths of each member and build a future of prosperity and abundance."

The crowd listens intently, their faces reflecting a mix of curiosity and hope.

"Trade agreements," Kato explains, "are formal agreements between countries that govern the terms of trade in goods, services, and investments. These agreements can take various forms, including free trade agreements, customs unions, and economic partnerships, and are often designed to reduce barriers to trade, promote economic integration, and enhance cooperation among member states."

He gestures to the nearby map, where lines blur between nations united in common purpose. "In Ndola, we recognize the importance of trade agreements and regional integration in promoting economic growth and development. From the Southern African Development Community (SADC) to the African Continental Free Trade Area (AfCFTA), these partnerships provide opportunities for our region to strengthen economic ties, increase market access, and attract investment."

Kato then turns his attention to the benefits of regional integration. "Regional integration," he explains, "is the process by which neighboring countries come together to deepen economic cooperation, harmonize policies, and promote regional development. By pooling resources, sharing infrastructure, and coordinating policies, regional integration can create economies of scale, enhance competitiveness, and stimulate trade and investment within the region."

A curious student named Fatima raises her hand. "But how do trade agreements and regional integration benefit ordinary citizens? Are there any challenges to overcome in achieving deeper economic integration?"

Kato's expression softens with empathy. "Ah, Fatima, an important question indeed. Trade agreements and regional integration can have significant benefits for ordinary citizens, including increased market access, expanded opportunities for employment and entrepreneurship, and higher standards of living. By facilitating the flow of goods, services, and investments, these agreements can stimulate economic growth, create jobs, and improve the welfare of communities."

He shares stories of countries that have embraced regional integration to overcome common challenges and achieve shared prosperity. "Take the European Union, for example," Kato says, nodding to the bloc's achievements. "Through its commitment to economic integration and cooperation, the EU has transformed Europe into a dynamic economic powerhouse, fostering peace, stability, and prosperity for its member states."

The audience nods in agreement, their faces reflecting a sense of understanding and determination.

Kato concludes with a call to action. "Let us embrace trade agreements and regional integration as instruments for building a future of shared prosperity and opportunity, committed to working together to overcome challenges, seize opportunities, and create a better world for ourselves and future generations."

As the session draws to a close, the crowd is filled with a renewed sense of hope and unity. With cooperation as their compass and collaboration as their guide, they disperse into the day, ready to embrace the opportunities of trade agreements and regional integration with confidence and determination.

Kato watches them go, his heart swelling with pride. He knows that with determination as their currency and solidarity as their strength, the residents of Ndola can harness the power of cooperation to build a future of prosperity and abundance for themselves and their community.

Trade Wars and Protectionism in the Modern Era

"Navigating Turbulent Waters: Understanding Trade Wars and Protectionism"

As the sun sets over Ndola, Kato returns to the community center, ready to delve into the complexities of trade wars and protectionism in the modern era. The air is thick with anticipation as the residents gather once more, eager to unravel the dynamics of global trade tensions and their impact on local economies.

Kato stands before the assembled crowd, his voice projecting a sense of urgency and concern. "Good evening, my friends. Today, we confront a pressing issue in the world of economics—trade wars and protectionism. In an era marked by rising tensions and shifting alliances, it is crucial that we understand the implications of these developments on our economy and our community. Together, we shall navigate the turbulent waters of global trade and emerge stronger and more resilient."

He begins with a solemn reflection. "In the intricate web of international relations, trade wars are the storms that threaten to disrupt the flow of global commerce, jeopardizing economies and livelihoods in their wake. Protectionism, driven by nationalist sentiments and economic anxieties, erects barriers to trade and stifles the spirit of cooperation that underpins prosperity. But let us not succumb to fear and uncertainty, for within these challenges lie the opportunities to forge new alliances, diversify our economies, and build resilience in the face of adversity."

The crowd listens intently, their faces reflecting a mix of concern and determination.

"Trade wars," Kato explains, "are conflicts between nations characterized by retaliatory tariffs, import restrictions, and other trade barriers. These conflicts can arise from disputes over trade practices, intellectual property rights, or geopolitical tensions, and can have far-reaching consequences for global supply chains, investment flows, and economic growth."

He gestures to the nearby market, where merchants exchange worried glances amidst rumors of impending tariffs and sanctions. "In Ndola, we are not immune to the effects of trade wars and protectionism. From higher prices for imported goods to reduced market access for our exports, these developments can disrupt our economy and threaten the livelihoods of our citizens."

Kato then turns his attention to the dangers of protectionism. "Protectionism," he explains, "refers to the policy of shielding domestic industries from foreign competition through tariffs, quotas, and subsidies. While protectionist measures may offer short-term relief for domestic producers, they can also lead to higher prices for consumers, reduced efficiency, and retaliation from trading partners, ultimately harming economic growth and prosperity for all."

A concerned farmer named Alice raises her hand. "But how can we protect our economy from the negative effects of trade wars and protectionism? Are there any strategies for mitigating the risks and promoting economic resilience?"

Kato's expression softens with empathy. "Ah, Alice, a critical question indeed. While we may not have control over the actions of other nations, there are steps we can take to safeguard our economy and build resilience in the face of trade wars and protectionism. By diversifying our export markets, investing in innovation and technology, and strengthening our domestic industries, we can reduce our reliance on any single market and mitigate the impact of trade disruptions."

He shares stories of communities that have weathered the storms of trade wars through unity, innovation, and adaptation. "By remaining vigilant, proactive, and united in our efforts, we can navigate the challenges of global trade and emerge stronger and more resilient," Kato says, nodding to the crowd.

The audience nods in agreement, their faces reflecting a sense of determination and solidarity.

Kato concludes with a call to action. "Let us stand firm against the forces of protectionism and trade wars, committed to upholding the principles of openness, cooperation, and mutual benefit in our global economy. By embracing diversity, fostering innovation, and building partnerships, we can overcome the challenges of today and create a brighter future for ourselves and future generations."

As the session draws to a close, the crowd is filled with a renewed sense of purpose and resolve. With unity as their shield and resilience as their armor, they disperse into the night, ready to confront the challenges of trade wars and protectionism with courage and determination.

Kato watches them go, his heart swelling with pride. He knows that with perseverance as their currency and solidarity as their strength, the residents of Ndola can navigate the turbulent waters of global trade and build a future of prosperity and resilience for themselves and their community.

7

Chapter 7: Public Finance and Fiscal Policy

The Economics of Taxation

"Balancing Acts: Exploring the Economics of Taxation"

In the heart of Ndola, amidst the hustle and bustle of daily life, Kato returns to the community center, ready to unravel the complexities of public finance and fiscal policy. The air is charged with anticipation as the residents gather once more, eager to understand the intricate dance between taxation, government spending, and economic stability.

Kato stands before the assembled crowd, his voice resonating with authority and clarity. "Good morning, my friends. Today, we embark on a journey into the world of public finance and fiscal policy—a realm where governments wield the power to tax and spend, shaping the economic landscape and influencing the lives of their citizens. But fear not, for together, we shall unravel the mysteries of taxation and explore the pathways to economic prosperity and social justice."

He begins with a reflective tone. "In the tapestry of public finance, taxation is the thread that binds society together, funding essential services, redistributing wealth, and shaping economic behavior. But let us not be daunted by its complexity, for within the principles of taxation lie the keys to building a fair and prosperous society for all."

The crowd listens intently, their faces reflecting a mix of curiosity and concern.

"The economics of taxation," Kato explains, "is the study of how taxes affect economic behavior, resource allocation, and overall welfare in society. Taxes can take various forms, including income taxes, sales taxes, property taxes, and corporate taxes, and are levied by governments to raise revenue, redistribute income, and achieve social and economic objectives."

He gestures to the nearby marketplace, where merchants tally their earnings and calculate their tax liabilities. "In Ndola, we are no strangers to the impact of taxation on our daily lives. From the taxes we pay on our income and purchases to the fees we contribute for public services and infrastructure, taxation plays a crucial role in funding government activities and shaping our economy."

Kato then turns his attention to the principles of taxation. "Taxation," he explains, "should be guided by principles of equity, efficiency, and simplicity. Equity requires that taxes be distributed fairly, with those who have more paying a higher share of their income. Efficiency requires that taxes minimize distortions to economic behavior, avoiding excessive burdens on productivity and investment. Simplicity requires that taxes be easy to understand, administer, and comply with, reducing compliance costs and administrative burdens for taxpayers."

A concerned citizen named Joseph raises his hand. "But how do taxes affect economic behavior and incentives? Are there any trade-offs to consider in designing tax policies?"

Kato's expression softens with empathy. "Ah, Joseph, an insightful question indeed. Taxes can influence economic behavior in various ways, affecting decisions about work, saving, investment, and consumption. Income taxes, for example, may reduce the incentive to work and save, while consumption taxes may encourage saving and investment. Tax policies must strike a balance between raising revenue for government activities and minimizing distortions to economic behavior, taking into account trade-offs between equity, efficiency, and simplicity."

He shares stories of countries that have implemented tax reforms to promote economic growth, reduce inequality, and enhance fiscal sustainability. "By designing tax policies that are fair, efficient, and transparent, governments can create a more equitable and prosperous society for all," Kato says, nodding to the crowd.

The audience nods in agreement, their faces reflecting a sense of understanding and determination.

Kato concludes with a call to action. "Let us embrace the economics of taxation as a tool for building a fair and prosperous society, committed to designing tax policies that promote equity, efficiency, and simplicity. By working together and engaging in informed dialogue, we can create a tax system that serves the needs of all citizens and fosters economic growth and social justice."

As the session draws to a close, the crowd is filled with a renewed sense of empowerment and purpose. With knowledge as their guide and collaboration as their strength, they disperse into the day, ready to engage in the ongoing conversation about taxation and public finance with newfound insight and understanding.

Kato watches them go, his heart swelling with pride. He knows that with determination as their currency and solidarity as their shield, the residents of Ndola can navigate the complexities of public finance and fiscal policy and build a future of prosperity and equity for themselves and their community.

Government Spending and Public Goods

"Investing in Communities: Government Spending and Public Goods"

As the sun reaches its zenith over Ndola, Kato returns to the community center, ready to delve deeper into the role of government spending and public goods in shaping the fabric of society. The atmosphere is alive with anticipation as the residents gather once more, eager to understand how public investments can improve their lives and strengthen their community.

Kato stands before the assembled crowd, his voice carrying a sense of purpose and conviction. "Good afternoon, my friends. Today, we continue our exploration of public finance and fiscal policy, focusing on the crucial role of government spending in providing essential services, infrastructure, and public goods. Together, we shall unravel the mysteries of public investment and explore the pathways to building resilient and thriving communities."

He begins with a contemplative reflection. "In the tapestry of public finance, government spending is the brushstroke that shapes the canvas of society, funding education, healthcare, transportation, and other vital services. But let us not overlook the significance of public goods—the bridges we cross, the parks we enjoy, the schools we attend—which bind us together as a community and enrich our lives in countless ways."

The crowd listens intently, their faces reflecting a mix of curiosity and anticipation.

"Government spending," Kato explains, "is the allocation of resources by public authorities to meet the needs and priorities of society. It encompasses a wide range of expenditures, including investments in infrastructure, social welfare programs, defense, and public administration. Government spending plays a crucial role in stimulating economic growth, reducing inequality, and fostering social cohesion."

He gestures to the nearby school, where children gather to learn and play. "In Ndola, we recognize the importance of government spending in providing essential services and infrastructure for our community. From schools and hospitals to roads and utilities, these investments improve our quality of life, enhance our productivity, and create opportunities for prosperity."

Kato then turns his attention to public goods. "Public goods," he explains, "are goods and services that are non-excludable and non-rivalrous, meaning that they are available to all members of society and their consumption by one individual does not diminish the availability of the good for others.

Examples of public goods include clean air, national defense, and public parks."

A concerned parent named Grace raises her hand. "But how does government spending on public goods benefit our community? Are there any challenges to consider in providing and funding these essential services?"

Kato's expression softens with empathy. "Ah, Grace, an important question indeed. Government spending on public goods benefits our community in many ways, from providing access to essential services and infrastructure to promoting social cohesion and environmental sustainability. However, there are challenges to consider in providing and funding these services, including competing priorities, limited resources, and the need for efficient and accountable governance."

He shares stories of communities that have leveraged public investment to improve living standards, create economic opportunities, and enhance quality of life for their citizens. "By prioritizing investments in public goods and fostering partnerships with the private sector and civil society, governments can address the needs and aspirations of their citizens and build a future of shared prosperity and well-being," Kato says, nodding to the crowd.

The audience nods in agreement, their faces reflecting a sense of understanding and determination.

Kato concludes with a call to action. "Let us embrace government spending as a catalyst for positive change, committed to investing in the well-being and prosperity of our community. By working together and engaging in informed dialogue, we can ensure that public investments reflect the needs and priorities of all citizens and contribute to building a brighter future for ourselves and future generations."

As the session draws to a close, the crowd is filled with a renewed sense of optimism and unity. With collaboration as their compass and resilience as their guide, they disperse into the afternoon, ready to engage in the ongoing conversation about government spending and public goods with renewed enthusiasm and determination.

Kato watches them go, his heart swelling with pride. He knows that with determination as their currency and solidarity as their strength, the residents of Ndola can harness the power of public investment to build a future of prosperity and well-being for themselves and their community.

Budget Deficits and National Debt

"Navigating Financial Waters: Understanding Budget Deficits and National Debt"

As twilight descends upon Ndola, Kato returns to the community center, ready to unravel the complexities of budget deficits and national debt. The air is filled with anticipation as the residents gather once more, eager to grasp the implications of these fiscal challenges and explore pathways to financial stability.

Kato stands before the assembled crowd, his voice resonating with solemnity and determination. "Good evening, my friends. Today, we confront a pressing issue in the realm of public finance—budget deficits and national debt. In an era marked by economic uncertainties and fiscal challenges, it is crucial that we understand the implications of these phenomena on our economy and our community. Together, we shall navigate the financial waters and emerge stronger and more resilient."

He begins with a reflective tone. "In the tapestry of public finance, budget deficits are the cracks that threaten to undermine the foundation of our economy, representing the shortfall between government revenues and expenditures. National debt, on the other hand, is the burden that weighs heavily on future generations, stemming from accumulated deficits over time. But let us not succumb to despair, for within these challenges lie the opportunities to build a future of fiscal responsibility and economic prosperity."

The crowd listens intently, their faces reflecting a mix of concern and resolve.

"Budget deficits," Kato explains, "occur when government spending exceeds government revenues in a given fiscal period, resulting in the need to borrow to finance the shortfall. While deficits may be necessary to stimulate economic growth, fund essential services, or address emergencies, persistent deficits can lead to unsustainable levels of national debt and pose risks to long-term fiscal health."

He gestures to the nearby market, where merchants tally their earnings amidst whispers of economic uncertainty. "In Ndola, we are not immune to the challenges of budget deficits and national debt. From the impact on government services and social programs to the burden on future generations, these fiscal challenges can affect our economy and our community in profound ways."

Kato then turns his attention to the implications of national debt. "National debt," he explains, "represents the accumulation of deficits over time, financed through borrowing from domestic and international creditors. While debt can be a useful tool for financing investments and smoothing consumption, excessive debt levels can undermine economic stability, crowd out private investment, and impose burdens on future generations."

A concerned citizen named David raises his hand. "But how can we address budget deficits and reduce national debt? Are there any strategies for achieving fiscal sustainability and ensuring the well-being of our community?"

Kato's expression softens with empathy. "Ah, David, an important question indeed. Addressing budget deficits and reducing national debt require a combination of prudent fiscal management, responsible budgeting, and structural reforms. Governments can pursue policies to enhance revenue generation, control spending, and prioritize investments that yield long-term benefits for society. By fostering economic growth, improving efficiency in government operations, and implementing measures to strengthen fiscal institutions, we can achieve fiscal sustainability and safeguard the well-being of our community."

He shares stories of countries that have successfully navigated fiscal challenges through sound fiscal policies, transparent governance, and strong political leadership. "By working together and embracing the principles of fiscal responsibility, we can build a future of financial stability and prosperity for ourselves and future generations," Kato says, nodding to the crowd.

The audience nods in agreement, their faces reflecting a sense of understanding and determination.

Kato concludes with a call to action. "Let us embrace the challenges of budget deficits and national debt as opportunities for growth and renewal, committed to fostering fiscal sustainability and ensuring the well-being of our community. By working together and engaging in informed dialogue, we can build a future where fiscal responsibility is the cornerstone of our prosperity and resilience."

As the session draws to a close, the crowd is filled with a renewed sense of purpose and resolve. With determination as their compass and unity as their strength, they disperse into the night, ready to confront the challenges of budget deficits and national debt with courage and determination.

Kato watches them go, his heart swelling with pride. He knows that with perseverance as their currency and solidarity as their shield, the residents of Ndola can navigate the financial waters and build a future of prosperity and well-being for themselves and their community.

Tax Incidence and Equity

"Fair Shares: Exploring Tax Incidence and Equity"

As dawn breaks over Ndola, Kato returns to the community center, ready to delve into the intricate dynamics of tax incidence and equity. The air is charged with anticipation as the residents gather once more, eager to understand how taxation affects different segments of society and how to ensure fairness in the distribution of tax burdens.

Kato stands before the assembled crowd, his voice resonating with empathy and determination. "Good morning, my friends. Today, we embark on a journey into the realm of tax incidence and equity—a realm where fairness and justice intersect with the complexities of taxation. Together, we shall explore the intricacies of who bears the burden of taxes and how to ensure that our tax system promotes equity and social cohesion."

He begins with a contemplative reflection. "In the tapestry of taxation, tax incidence is the pattern that emerges, revealing who ultimately bears the burden of taxes—whether it be consumers, producers, or workers. Equity, on the other hand, is the guiding principle that ensures fairness and justice in the distribution of tax burdens. But let us not be daunted by the complexities of tax policy, for within these challenges lie the opportunities to create a tax system that promotes social justice and economic well-being for all."

The crowd listens intently, their faces reflecting a mix of curiosity and concern.

"Tax incidence," Kato explains, "refers to the distribution of the burden of taxes across different segments of society. While taxes may be levied on businesses or individuals, the ultimate incidence of taxes depends on factors such as the elasticity of demand and supply, market structures, and the mobility of factors of production. Understanding tax incidence is crucial for designing tax policies that are equitable, efficient, and conducive to economic growth."

He gestures to the nearby marketplace, where merchants negotiate prices amidst whispers of tax hikes and adjustments. "In Ndola, we recognize the importance of tax policy in promoting social justice and economic development. From progressive income taxes that ensure the wealthy contribute their fair share to consumption taxes that may disproportionately affect low-income households, tax policy can have profound implications for equity and fairness in our society."

Kato then turns his attention to the principles of equity in taxation. "Equity," he explains, "requires that taxes be distributed fairly, with those who have more paying a higher share of their income or wealth. Progressive taxation, which imposes higher tax rates on higher-income earners, is one approach to promoting equity and redistributing income. However, achieving equity in taxation requires careful consideration of the impact of taxes on different segments of society and the need to balance competing objectives such as economic efficiency and administrative simplicity."

A concerned citizen named Sarah raises her hand. "But how can we ensure that our tax system is fair and equitable? Are there any challenges to consider in promoting tax equity?"

Kato's expression softens with empathy. "Ah, Sarah, an important question indeed. Ensuring tax equity requires a multifaceted approach that involves designing tax policies that are progressive, transparent, and accountable. Governments can use a combination of direct and indirect taxes, tax credits and deductions, and targeted social programs to promote equity and mitigate the impact of taxes on vulnerable populations. However, challenges such as tax evasion, loopholes, and administrative inefficiencies must be addressed to ensure that our tax system promotes fairness and justice for all."

He shares stories of countries that have implemented progressive tax policies and social safety nets to promote equity and reduce income inequality. "By working together and engaging in informed dialogue, we can build a tax system that reflects our values of fairness, justice, and compassion," Kato says, nodding to the crowd.

The audience nods in agreement, their faces reflecting a sense of understanding and determination.

Kato concludes with a call to action. "Let us embrace tax incidence and equity as guiding principles in our quest for a fairer and more just society, committed to building a tax system that promotes social cohesion and economic prosperity for all. By working together and advocating for positive change, we can create a future where everyone pays their fair share and no one is left behind."

As the session draws to a close, the crowd is filled with a renewed sense of purpose and solidarity. With determination as their compass and equity as their guide, they disperse into the day, ready to advocate for a tax system that promotes fairness and justice for themselves and future generations.

Kato watches them go, his heart swelling with pride. He knows that with perseverance as their currency and solidarity as their strength, the residents of Ndola can navigate the complexities of tax policy and build a future of prosperity and equity for themselves and their community.

Fiscal Policy Tools and Economic Stabilization

"Steering the Ship: Harnessing Fiscal Policy for Economic Stability"

As the sun dips below the horizon in Ndola, Kato returns to the community center, ready to explore the tools of fiscal policy and their role in steering the economy towards stability. The atmosphere is charged with anticipation as the residents gather once more, eager to understand how government policies can mitigate economic fluctuations and promote prosperity for all.

Kato stands before the assembled crowd, his voice filled with determination and purpose. "Good evening, my friends. Today, we continue our journey through the realm of public finance, focusing on the powerful tools of fiscal policy and their role in stabilizing the economy. Together, we shall unravel the complexities of government intervention and explore the pathways to economic stability and prosperity."

He begins with a contemplative reflection. "In the tumultuous seas of economic uncertainty, fiscal policy serves as the compass that guides our course, providing direction and stability in times of turbulence. But let us not be overwhelmed by the challenges ahead, for within the arsenal of fiscal policy lie the tools to navigate the storms of recession, inflation, and unemployment."

The crowd listens intently, their faces reflecting a mix of curiosity and concern.

"Fiscal policy," Kato explains, "refers to the use of government spending and taxation to influence the level of economic activity and achieve macroeconomic objectives such as full employment, price stability, and sustainable growth. Governments can use a combination of expansionary and contractionary fiscal policies to address fluctuations in aggregate demand and stabilize the economy."

He gestures to the nearby market, where merchants adjust their strategies amidst whispers of economic downturns and uncertainties. "In Ndola, we recognize the importance of fiscal policy in promoting economic stability and prosperity. From infrastructure investments and social welfare programs to tax incentives and stimulus measures, fiscal policy can play a crucial role in supporting businesses, creating jobs, and restoring confidence in the economy."

Kato then turns his attention to the tools of fiscal policy. "Expansionary fiscal policy," he explains, "involves increasing government spending or reducing taxes to boost aggregate demand and stimulate economic growth. This approach is often used during periods of recession or economic downturns to spur investment, consumption, and employment. Conversely, contractionary fiscal policy involves decreasing government spending or raising taxes to curb inflation and prevent overheating of the economy."

A concerned business owner named James raises his hand. "But how effective are these fiscal policy tools in stabilizing the economy? Are there any limitations or challenges to consider in their implementation?"

Kato's expression softens with empathy. "Ah, James, an important question indeed. The effectiveness of fiscal policy tools depends on various factors, including the responsiveness of economic agents to changes in government policies, the timing and magnitude of fiscal interventions, and the presence of other macroeconomic shocks or constraints. Additionally, there are limitations and challenges to consider in the implementation of fiscal policy, such as political constraints, budgetary constraints, and the risk of unintended consequences."

He shares stories of countries that have successfully used fiscal policy to navigate economic crises and promote long-term growth and stability. "By adopting a proactive and pragmatic approach to fiscal policy, governments can help steer the economy towards prosperity and resilience," Kato says, nodding to the crowd.

The audience nods in agreement, their faces reflecting a sense of understanding and determination.

Kato concludes with a call to action. "Let us embrace fiscal policy as a powerful tool for economic stabilization and prosperity, committed to using our collective resources and ingenuity to build a future of shared prosperity and well-being for all. By working together and advocating for sound economic policies, we can navigate the challenges ahead and create a brighter future for ourselves and future generations."

As the session draws to a close, the crowd is filled with a renewed sense of hope and solidarity. With determination as their compass and collaboration as their strength, they disperse into the night, ready to engage in the ongoing conversation about fiscal policy and economic stability with renewed enthusiasm and determination.

Kato watches them go, his heart swelling with pride. He knows that with perseverance as their currency and solidarity as their shield, the residents of Ndola can harness the power of fiscal policy to build a future of prosperity and resilience for themselves and their community.

Debates in Public Finance: Austerity vs. Stimulus

"Balancing Acts: Navigating the Austerity vs. Stimulus Debate"

As the sun rises over Ndola, Kato returns to the community center, prepared to delve into the contentious debate surrounding austerity and stimulus measures in public finance. The atmosphere crackles with anticipation as the residents gather once more, eager to understand the competing ideologies and their implications for economic policy.

Kato stands before the assembled crowd, his voice projecting a sense of gravitas and urgency. "Good morning, my friends. Today, we confront a fundamental debate in the realm of public finance—the age-old question of austerity versus stimulus. In an era marked by economic uncertainties and fiscal challenges, it is crucial that we understand the competing ideologies and their impact on our economy and our community. Together, we shall navigate the complexities of this debate and seek pathways to economic stability and prosperity."

He begins with a contemplative tone. "In the landscape of economic policy, austerity and stimulus represent two divergent approaches to fiscal management. Austerity advocates for fiscal restraint, emphasizing the need to reduce government spending and balance budgets to restore confidence in the economy and promote long-term sustainability. Stimulus, on the other hand, calls for government intervention to boost demand and support economic growth through increased spending and tax cuts. But let us not be swayed by ideology alone, for within this debate lie nuanced considerations and real-world implications for our society."

The crowd listens intently, their faces reflecting a mix of curiosity and concern.

"Austerity," Kato explains, "is often championed as a necessary measure to address fiscal imbalances, reduce public debt, and restore investor confidence. Proponents argue that by tightening fiscal belts and implementing structural reforms, governments can lay the groundwork for sustainable economic growth and prosperity in the long run. However, austerity measures can also lead to social dislocation, economic hardship, and exacerbate inequalities, particularly for vulnerable populations."

He gestures to the nearby market, where merchants discuss the impact of budget cuts and spending constraints on their businesses. "In Ndola, we have witnessed the consequences of austerity measures on our community—from cuts to public services and social programs to layoffs and unemployment. While austerity may offer short-term solutions to fiscal challenges, it can also have long-lasting implications for our economy and our society."

Kato then turns his attention to stimulus measures. "Stimulus," he explains, "advocates for government intervention to boost demand, create jobs, and support economic recovery through increased spending on infrastructure, social programs, and tax cuts. Proponents argue that by injecting liquidity into the economy and stimulating consumer and business confidence, governments can catalyze growth and lay the foundation for long-term prosperity. However, stimulus measures can also lead to inflationary pressures, budget deficits, and concerns about the sustainability of public finances."

A concerned community leader named Esther raises her hand. "But how do we navigate the trade-offs between austerity and stimulus? Are there any lessons from history or best practices to guide our decision-making?"

Kato's expression softens with empathy. "Ah, Esther, a poignant question indeed. Navigating the debate between austerity and stimulus requires careful consideration of economic conditions, policy objectives, and societal needs. While there is no one-size-fits-all solution, history and empirical evidence offer valuable insights into the effectiveness and limitations of both approaches. In times of economic downturns or crises, stimulus measures may be necessary to kickstart growth and restore confidence. However, in periods of economic stability or overheating, austerity measures may be needed to ensure fiscal sustainability and prevent inflationary pressures."

He shares stories of countries that have successfully managed fiscal challenges through a balanced approach, combining austerity with targeted stimulus measures to achieve economic stability and prosperity. "By adopting a pragmatic and flexible approach to fiscal policy, governments can navigate the complexities of the austerity versus stimulus debate and build a future of resilience and prosperity for all," Kato says, nodding to the crowd.

The audience nods in agreement, their faces reflecting a sense of understanding and determination.

Kato concludes with a call to action. "Let us transcend the ideological divides of austerity and stimulus, committed to adopting policies that promote economic stability, social cohesion, and shared prosperity. By working together and engaging in informed dialogue, we can navigate the complexities of public finance and build a future where everyone has the opportunity to thrive and succeed."

As the session draws to a close, the crowd is filled with a renewed sense of purpose and solidarity. With determination as their compass and collaboration as their strength, they disperse into the day, ready to engage in the ongoing conversation about fiscal policy and economic governance with renewed enthusiasm and determination.

Kato watches them go, his heart swelling with pride. He knows that with perseverance as their currency and solidarity as their shield, the residents of Ndola can navigate the complexities of economic policy and build a future of prosperity and resilience for themselves and their community.

8

Chapter 8: Behavioral Economics

Psychological Foundations of Economic Behavior

"The Human Element: Unveiling the Psychological Foundations of Economic Behavior"

As the sun casts its golden glow over Ndola, Kato returns to the community center, prepared to unravel the intricate interplay between psychology and economics in shaping human behavior. The air is charged with curiosity and anticipation as the residents gather once more, eager to explore the hidden motivations behind economic decisions.

Kato stands before the assembled crowd, his voice resonating with warmth and wisdom. "Good afternoon, my friends. Today, we embark on a fascinating journey into the realm of behavioral economics—a discipline that seeks to understand how human psychology influences economic decision-making. Together, we shall peel back the layers of the human mind and discover the hidden drivers behind our economic behaviors."

He begins with a reflective tone. "In the tapestry of economic theory, traditional models often assume that individuals are rational actors, making decisions based on careful analysis and self-interest. However, behavioral economics challenges this assumption, revealing the rich tapestry of human cognition, emotion, and social influences that shape our economic choices. But let us not be daunted by the complexities of the human psyche, for within the realm of behavioral economics lie profound insights into the mysteries of human behavior."

The crowd listens intently, their faces reflecting a mix of intrigue and wonder.

"Psychological foundations," Kato explains, "underpin our economic behaviors, influencing how we perceive risks, evaluate gains and losses, and make decisions under uncertainty. From cognitive biases and heuristics to social norms and emotions, these psychological factors shape our preferences, beliefs, and attitudes towards risk and reward."

He gestures to the nearby marketplace, where traders negotiate prices amidst whispers of uncertainty and speculation. "In Ndola, we are no strangers to the complexities of human behavior in economic transactions. From the fear of loss driving investment decisions to the influence of social norms on consumption patterns, the psychological foundations of economic behavior are ever-present in our daily lives."

Kato then turns his attention to cognitive biases. "Cognitive biases," he explains, "are systematic errors in thinking that lead to irrational decision-making. From the tendency to overvalue immediate gains and undervalue future rewards to the aversion to losses and the herd mentality, cognitive biases can lead individuals to make suboptimal decisions in economic contexts."

A curious young student named Mwansa raises her hand. "But how do these cognitive biases affect economic outcomes? Are there any strategies for mitigating their impact on decision-making?"

Kato's expression softens with empathy. "Ah, Mwansa, an insightful question indeed. Cognitive biases can have profound implications for economic outcomes, leading to market inefficiencies, asset bubbles, and financial crises. However, by raising awareness of these biases and implementing decision-making strategies such as nudges, defaults, and incentives, individuals and policymakers can mitigate their impact and promote more rational economic behaviors."

He shares stories of behavioral interventions that have successfully influenced economic decision-making, from retirement savings programs to environmental conservation initiatives. "By understanding the psychological foundations of economic behavior and applying behavioral insights to policy design, we can create a more informed and compassionate society," Kato says, nodding to the crowd.

The audience nods in agreement, their faces reflecting a sense of understanding and empowerment.

Kato concludes with a call to action. "Let us embrace the insights of behavioral economics as a lens through which to understand and address the complexities of human behavior in economic contexts. By working together and engaging in informed dialogue, we can harness the power of psychology to build a future where economic decisions are guided by wisdom, compassion, and foresight."

As the session draws to a close, the crowd is filled with a renewed sense of curiosity and determination. With knowledge as their compass and empathy as their guide, they disperse into the evening, ready to explore the hidden depths of human behavior and build a future of prosperity and understanding for themselves and their community.

Kato watches them go, his heart swelling with pride. He knows that with curiosity as their currency and compassion as their strength, the residents of Ndola can navigate the complexities of behavioral economics and unlock the potential for a brighter future.

Prospect Theory and Decision-Making Biases

"Navigating the Mind: Unraveling Prospect Theory and Decision-Making Biases"

As the moon rises over Ndola, Kato returns to the community center, ready to delve deeper into the realm of behavioral economics. The air is thick with anticipation as the residents gather once more, eager to uncover the nuances of decision-making biases and their impact on economic choices.

Kato stands before the assembled crowd, his voice carrying a sense of intrigue and exploration. "Good evening, my friends. Today, we continue our exploration of behavioral economics, focusing on Prospect Theory and the myriad biases that influence our decision-making. Together, we shall navigate the labyrinth of the human mind and discover the hidden forces that shape our economic choices."

He begins with a contemplative reflection. "In the realm of economic decision-making, traditional models often assume that individuals weigh the potential gains and losses of their choices with perfect rationality. However, Prospect Theory challenges this assumption, revealing the asymmetrical way in which we perceive risks and rewards. But let us not be daunted by the complexities of human cognition, for within the realm of Prospect Theory lie profound insights into the quirks and foibles of the human psyche."

The crowd listens intently, their faces reflecting a mix of curiosity and fascination.

"Prospect Theory," Kato explains, "proposes that individuals evaluate potential outcomes relative to a reference point, such as their current wealth or status quo. Loss aversion, one of the key tenets of Prospect Theory, suggests that individuals are more sensitive to losses than to equivalent gains, leading to risk aversion and suboptimal decision-making in economic contexts."

He gestures to the nearby marketplace, where traders weigh the risks and rewards of their investments amidst whispers of uncertainty and speculation. "In Ndola, we see the manifestations of Prospect Theory in our everyday lives—from the reluctance to sell investments at a loss to the tendency to hold onto losing positions in the hope of a rebound. These decision-making biases can have profound implications for our financial well-being and the stability of our economy."

Kato then turns his attention to other decision-making biases. "Beyond loss aversion," he explains, "there are a multitude of cognitive biases that influence our economic choices. From the availability heuristic, which leads us to overestimate the likelihood of events based on their salience in memory, to confirmation bias, which causes us to seek out information that confirms our preexisting beliefs, these biases can lead to suboptimal decisions and market inefficiencies."

A concerned business owner named Patrick raises his hand.

"But how do we overcome these decision-making biases? Are there any strategies for mitigating their impact on economic outcomes?"

Kato's expression softens with empathy. "Ah, Patrick, an important question indeed. Overcoming decision-making biases requires awareness, education, and the implementation of decision-making strategies that promote rationality and mindfulness. By recognizing our cognitive biases and employing techniques such as decision framing, diversification, and deliberate thinking, we can mitigate their impact and make more informed economic choices."

He shares stories of individuals and organizations that have successfully navigated decision-making biases to achieve their goals and aspirations. "By embracing the insights of Prospect Theory and behavioral economics, we can unlock the potential for wiser and more prudent decision-making," Kato says, nodding to the crowd.

The audience nods in agreement, their faces reflecting a sense of understanding and empowerment.

Kato concludes with a call to action. "Let us embrace the quirks and foibles of the human mind as opportunities for growth and self-improvement. By working together and engaging in informed dialogue, we can harness the power of behavioral economics to build a future where economic choices are guided by wisdom, insight, and compassion."

As the session draws to a close, the crowd is filled with a renewed sense of curiosity and determination. With knowledge as their compass and mindfulness as their guide, they disperse into the night, ready to apply the insights of Prospect Theory and decision-making biases to their lives and communities.

Kato watches them go, his heart swelling with pride. He

knows that with awareness as their currency and resilience as their strength, the residents of Ndola can navigate the complexities of the human mind and build a future of prosperity and well-being for themselves and their community.

Nudge Theory and Behavioral Interventions

"Guiding Light: Harnessing Nudge Theory and Behavioral Interventions"

As dawn breaks over Ndola, Kato returns to the community center, prepared to explore the transformative power of nudge theory and behavioral interventions. The air is charged with anticipation as the residents gather once more, eager to discover how subtle nudges can shape their economic decisions.

Kato stands before the assembled crowd, his voice carrying a sense of optimism and possibility. "Good morning, my friends. Today, we delve into the realm of nudge theory and behavioral interventions—a realm where small changes can lead to big impacts on economic behavior. Together, we shall uncover the gentle nudges that guide our choices and shape our economic destinies."

He begins with a contemplative reflection. "In the tapestry of behavioral economics, nudge theory proposes that subtle changes in the presentation of choices can influence our decisions without restricting our freedom of choice. But let us not underestimate the power of these gentle nudges, for within them lie the potential to promote healthier, wealthier, and happier lives."

The crowd listens intently, their faces reflecting a mix of

curiosity and intrigue.

"Nudge theory," Kato explains, "recognizes that human beings are susceptible to cognitive biases and decision-making heuristics, often leading to suboptimal choices. By designing choice architectures that make desirable options more salient, accessible, and attractive, policymakers and organizations can gently steer individuals towards better outcomes without resorting to mandates or restrictions."

He gestures to the nearby marketplace, where merchants display healthier food options amidst whispers of encouragement and support. "In Ndola, we see the application of nudge theory in various aspects of our lives—from promoting healthier lifestyles and sustainable behaviors to encouraging savings and retirement planning. These subtle interventions can have profound impacts on our well-being and the vitality of our community."

Kato then turns his attention to examples of behavioral interventions. "Beyond nudge theory," he explains, "there are a myriad of behavioral interventions that can influence economic behavior and decision-making. From defaults that encourage participation in beneficial programs to personalized feedback that enhances self-awareness and motivation, these interventions leverage insights from psychology to promote positive change."

A curious young mother named Mary raises her hand. "But how do these behavioral interventions work? Are there any examples of their effectiveness in real-world settings?"

Kato's expression softens with empathy. "Ah, Mary, an insightful question indeed. Behavioral interventions work by leveraging principles of psychology to influence behavior in subtle yet meaningful ways. For example, studies have shown that changing the default option for retirement savings from opt-in to opt-out can significantly increase participation rates, leading to higher savings and financial security in retirement."

He shares stories of successful behavioral interventions in diverse settings, from encouraging energy conservation to promoting charitable giving and tax compliance. "By harnessing the power of nudges and behavioral interventions, we can create environments that make it easier for individuals to make healthier, wealthier, and happier choices," Kato says, nodding to the crowd.

The audience nods in agreement, their faces reflecting a sense of understanding and empowerment.

Kato concludes with a call to action. "Let us embrace the gentle nudges and behavioral interventions that guide us towards better economic outcomes and brighter futures. By working together and engaging in informed dialogue, we can harness the power of behavioral economics to build a future where choices are guided by wisdom, compassion, and foresight."

As the session draws to a close, the crowd is filled with a renewed sense of optimism and determination. With nudges as their guide and collaboration as their strength, they disperse into the day, ready to apply the insights of nudge theory and behavioral interventions to their lives and communities.

Kato watches them go, his heart swelling with pride. He knows that with nudges as their compass and resilience as their strength, the residents of Ndola can navigate the complexities of economic decision-making and build a future of prosperity and well-being for themselves and their community.

The Role of Emotions in Economic Choices

"Heart and Mind: Exploring the Role of Emotions in Economic Choices"

As the sun sets over Ndola, Kato returns to the community center, prepared to delve into the complex interplay between emotions and economic decision-making. The atmosphere is filled with intrigue and curiosity as the residents gather once more, eager to uncover the hidden influences that shape their choices.

Kato stands before the assembled crowd, his voice carrying a sense of empathy and understanding. "Good evening, my friends. Today, we embark on a journey into the realm of emotions and their profound impact on our economic decisions. Together, we shall unravel the mysteries of the human heart and discover how our emotions shape the pathways of prosperity and well-being."

He begins with a contemplative reflection. "In the tapestry of economic behavior, traditional models often overlook the role of emotions, assuming that individuals make decisions based solely on rationality and self-interest. However, emotions play a crucial role in shaping our perceptions, preferences, and behaviors, often leading us to make choices that defy logic or reason. But let us not dismiss the power of emotions, for within them lie the seeds of inspiration, connection, and meaning."

The crowd listens intently, their faces reflecting a mix of curiosity and introspection.

"Emotions," Kato explains, "influence our economic choices in profound ways, coloring our perceptions of risks and rewards, guiding our preferences, and shaping our attitudes towards uncertainty. From the fear of loss driving investment decisions to the joy of generosity motivating charitable giving, emotions can lead us down unexpected paths and shape the contours of our economic destinies."

He gestures to the nearby marketplace, where traders negotiate prices amidst whispers of excitement and apprehension. "In Ndola, we witness the ebbs and flows of emotions in our economic transactions—from the exuberance of a successful business venture to the despair of financial hardship. These emotional experiences can influence our decisions in subtle yet profound ways, often leading us to prioritize short-term gratification over long-term goals or succumb to impulses that defy rationality."

Kato then turns his attention to the role of emotional intelligence. "Beyond the influence of emotions," he explains, "lies the potential for emotional intelligence—a capacity to recognize, understand, and manage our emotions in ways that promote well-being and wise decision-making. By cultivating emotional awareness and resilience, individuals can navigate the complexities of economic choices with greater clarity, compassion, and purpose."

A concerned community leader named Esther raises her hand. "But how do we cultivate emotional intelligence? Are there any strategies for managing our emotions in economic contexts?"

Kato's expression softens with empathy. "Ah, Esther, a poignant question indeed. Cultivating emotional intelligence requires self-reflection, empathy, and practice. By developing mindfulness techniques, such as meditation and deep breathing, individuals can cultivate emotional awareness and regulation, allowing them to navigate the ups and downs of economic life with greater equanimity and insight."

He shares stories of individuals who have successfully managed their emotions in economic contexts, from entrepreneurs who have overcome setbacks to investors who have remained resilient in the face of market volatility. "By embracing the power of emotions and cultivating emotional intelligence, we can transform our economic choices from moments of uncertainty to opportunities for growth and self-discovery," Kato says, nodding to the crowd.

The audience nods in agreement, their faces reflecting a sense of understanding and empowerment.

Kato concludes with a call to action. "Let us embrace the richness of our emotions as guides on the journey of economic life. By working together and supporting one another in our emotional growth, we can build a future where economic choices are infused with wisdom, compassion, and authenticity."

As the session draws to a close, the crowd is filled with a renewed sense of connection and purpose. With emotions as their compass and resilience as their strength, they disperse into the night, ready to navigate the complexities of economic life with greater clarity and compassion.

Kato watches them go, his heart swelling with pride. He knows that with empathy as their guide and community as their support, the residents of Ndola can harness the power of emotions to create a future of prosperity and well-being for themselves and their community.

Behavioral Economics in Public Policy

"Shaping Tomorrow: Harnessing Behavioral Economics in Public Policy"

As dawn breaks over Ndola, Kato returns to the community center, ready to explore the transformative potential of behavioral economics in shaping public policy. The air is filled with anticipation as the residents gather once more, eager to discover how insights from human behavior can guide policies for the common good.

Kato stands before the assembled crowd, his voice resonating with determination and hope. "Good morning, my friends. Today, we embark on a journey into the realm of public policy, where the principles of behavioral economics offer new pathways to address social challenges and promote well-being for all. Together, we shall uncover the tools and strategies that policymakers can use to create a future of prosperity, equity, and justice."

He begins with a contemplative reflection. "In the arena of public policy, traditional approaches often rely on assumptions of rationality and self-interest, overlooking the complexities of human behavior. However, behavioral economics challenges these assumptions, revealing the irrationalities and biases that influence our decisions. But let us not despair, for within the realm of behavioral economics lie innovative solutions to age-old problems."

The crowd listens intently, their faces reflecting a mix of curiosity and determination.

"Behavioral economics," Kato explains, "offers policymakers a toolkit for designing interventions that nudge individuals towards better outcomes without restricting their freedom of choice. From improving public health outcomes to promoting environmental conservation and financial literacy, behavioral insights can inform policies that address the root causes of societal challenges and empower individuals to make healthier, wealthier, and happier choices."

He gestures to the nearby marketplace, where vendors discuss the impact of government policies on their businesses amidst whispers of optimism and concern. "In Ndola, we see the potential of behavioral economics in action—from campaigns that encourage vaccination and disease prevention to initiatives that promote energy conservation and sustainable development. These policies leverage insights from human behavior to create environments that make it easier for individuals to make choices that benefit themselves and society as a whole."

Kato then turns his attention to examples of behavioral interventions in public policy. "Beyond theory," he explains, "lie real-world examples of policies that have successfully incorporated behavioral insights to achieve positive outcomes. From automatic enrollment in retirement savings programs to personalized feedback on energy consumption, these interventions demonstrate the power of behavioral economics to inform policies that improve lives and build stronger communities."

A concerned citizen named Grace raises her hand. "But how do we ensure that policies informed by behavioral economics are ethical and equitable? Are there any considerations for protecting individual rights and promoting social justice?"

Kato's expression softens with empathy. "Ah, Grace, a crucial question indeed. Ensuring the ethical and equitable implementation of policies informed by behavioral economics requires transparency, accountability, and community engagement. By consulting with diverse stakeholders, conducting rigorous evaluations, and incorporating principles of fairness and justice into policy design, policymakers can create interventions that uphold individual rights and promote social well-being."

He shares stories of policymakers who have successfully navigated the complexities of behavioral economics to address social challenges and promote inclusive growth. "By embracing the insights of behavioral economics and collaborating with communities, governments can create a future where policies are guided by empathy, evidence, and equity," Kato says, nodding to the crowd.

The audience nods in agreement, their faces reflecting a sense of understanding and empowerment.

Kato concludes with a call to action. "Let us embrace the promise of behavioral economics as a catalyst for positive change in our communities and our world. By working together and advocating for policies that empower individuals and promote social justice, we can build a future where everyone has the opportunity to thrive and succeed."

As the session draws to a close, the crowd is filled with a renewed sense of purpose and solidarity. With behavioral economics as their compass and collaboration as their strength, they disperse into the day, ready to engage in the ongoing conversation about public policy with renewed enthusiasm and determination.

Kato watches them go, his heart swelling with pride. He knows that with empathy as their guide and community as their support, the residents of Ndola can harness the power of behavioral economics to create a future of prosperity and justice for themselves and their community.

Ethical Considerations in Behavioral Economics Research

"The Moral Compass: Navigating Ethical Considerations in Behavioral Economics Research"

As twilight descends over Ndola, Kato returns to the community center, ready to delve into the ethical dimensions of behavioral economics research. The atmosphere is tinged with introspection and contemplation as the residents gather once more, eager to explore the ethical implications of understanding human behavior.

Kato stands before the assembled crowd, his voice carrying a tone of solemnity and reflection. "Good evening, my friends. Today, we confront a crucial aspect of behavioral economics research—the ethical considerations that guide our exploration of human behavior. Together, we shall navigate the moral complexities that arise from our quest for knowledge and understanding."

He begins with a thoughtful reflection. "In the pursuit of knowledge, researchers in behavioral economics often grapple with ethical dilemmas and moral quandaries. From questions of consent and privacy to concerns about manipulation and exploitation, our exploration of human behavior must be guided by principles of integrity, respect, and empathy. But let us not shy away from these ethical challenges, for within them lie opportunities for growth, learning, and reflection."

The crowd listens intently, their faces reflecting a mix of

contemplation and concern.

"Ethical considerations," Kato explains, "are paramount in all stages of behavioral economics research, from the design and implementation of experiments to the dissemination of findings and their implications for policy and practice. Researchers must ensure that their studies uphold the principles of informed consent, privacy protection, and beneficence, safeguarding the well-being and dignity of participants at all times."

He gestures to the nearby marketplace, where vendors discuss the importance of trust and integrity in their business dealings amidst whispers of integrity and honesty. "In Ndola, we see the importance of ethical considerations in our daily lives—from the respect for individual autonomy and privacy to the recognition of the inherent dignity and worth of every person. These ethical principles must guide our research endeavors, ensuring that our pursuit of knowledge is rooted in compassion, fairness, and justice."

Kato then turns his attention to examples of ethical dilemmas in behavioral economics research. "Beyond theory," he explains, "lie real-world examples of researchers grappling with ethical dilemmas in their quest to understand human behavior. From experiments that challenge conventional norms to studies that raise questions about the limits of consent and autonomy, these dilemmas remind us of the complexities of the human experience and the importance of ethical reflection in our research endeavors."

A concerned student named David raises his hand. "But how do we navigate these ethical dilemmas? Are there any guidelines or frameworks for conducting ethical research in behavioral economics?"

Kato's expression softens with empathy. "Ah, David, a crucial question indeed. Navigating ethical dilemmas in behavioral economics research requires humility, transparency, and a commitment to ethical reflection. Researchers must engage in dialogue with stakeholders, seek guidance from ethical review boards, and adhere to established guidelines and codes of conduct, such as those outlined by professional associations and regulatory bodies."

He shares stories of researchers who have navigated ethical dilemmas with integrity and compassion, ensuring that their studies uphold the principles of respect, beneficence, and justice. "By embracing ethical considerations in our research endeavors, we can ensure that our pursuit of knowledge is guided by integrity, empathy, and a commitment to the common good," Kato says, nodding to the crowd.

The audience nods in agreement, their faces reflecting a sense of understanding and determination.

Kato concludes with a call to action. "Let us embrace the ethical dimensions of behavioral economics research as opportunities for growth, learning, and reflection. By working together and upholding the principles of integrity, respect, and compassion, we can build a future where our pursuit of knowledge is guided by wisdom, empathy, and a commitment to the well-being of all."

As the session draws to a close, the crowd is filled with a renewed sense of introspection and resolve. With ethics as their compass and integrity as their strength, they disperse into the night, ready to engage in the ongoing pursuit of knowledge with humility and compassion.

Kato watches them go, his heart swelling with pride. He knows that with empathy as their guide and integrity as their anchor, the residents of Ndola can navigate the complexities of behavioral economics research and build a future of ethical inquiry and moral reflection for themselves and their community.

9

Chapter 9: Innovation and Technological Change

The Economics of Innovation

"Pioneering Tomorrow: Unveiling the Economics of Innovation"

As the first rays of dawn illuminate Ndola, Kato returns to the community center, eager to explore the transformative power of innovation and technological change. The air is charged with anticipation as the residents gather once more, ready to embark on a journey into the heart of economic progress.

Kato stands before the assembled crowd, his voice infused with excitement and curiosity. "Good morning, my friends. Today, we delve into the dynamic realm of innovation and technological change—a realm where creativity, ingenuity, and perseverance converge to shape the future of our economy and society. Together, we shall unravel the mysteries of innovation and discover its profound impact on our lives and communities."

He begins with a reflective tone. "In the tapestry of economic progress, innovation plays a central role in driving growth, prosperity, and societal advancement. From the invention of the wheel to the advent of the internet, innovations have reshaped the way we live, work, and interact with the world around us. But let us not overlook the economic foundations of innovation, for within them lie the keys to unlocking human potential and building a brighter future."

The crowd listens intently, their faces reflecting a mix of awe and inspiration.

"The economics of innovation," Kato explains, "encompasses the processes by which new ideas, technologies, and business models are developed, diffused, and commercialized. It involves the interaction of diverse actors—entrepreneurs, inventors, investors, and policymakers—who collaborate to transform ideas into tangible products, services, and solutions that address unmet needs and create value for society."

He gestures to the nearby marketplace, where entrepreneurs showcase their latest inventions amidst whispers of excitement and anticipation. "In Ndola, we witness the spirit of innovation in action—from local artisans crafting handmade goods to tech startups developing cutting-edge solutions for sustainable agriculture and renewable energy. These innovations not only drive economic growth and job creation but also foster creativity, resilience, and community empowerment."

Kato then turns his attention to the importance of innovation ecosystems. "Beyond individual inventions," he explains, "lie innovation ecosystems—networks of institutions, resources, and supportive policies that nurture creativity, collaboration, and entrepreneurship. From research universities and incubators to venture capital firms and regulatory frameworks, these ecosystems provide the fertile ground upon which innovations can flourish and thrive."

A budding entrepreneur named Chanda raises her hand. "But how do we foster innovation in our community? Are there any strategies for creating a vibrant innovation ecosystem that supports entrepreneurs and inventors?"

Kato's expression brightens with enthusiasm. "Ah, Chanda, an insightful question indeed. Fostering innovation requires a multifaceted approach that addresses the diverse needs of innovators and entrepreneurs. By investing in education and skills development, supporting research and development initiatives, and fostering collaboration between industry and academia, communities can create a supportive environment where innovation can thrive."

He shares stories of successful innovation initiatives in diverse settings, from public-private partnerships that promote technology transfer to grassroots movements that empower local innovators and creators. "By embracing the economics of innovation and fostering a culture of creativity and collaboration, communities can unlock the potential for transformative change and build a future where innovation drives sustainable development and shared prosperity," Kato says, nodding to the crowd.

The audience nods in agreement, their faces reflecting a sense of determination and hope.

Kato concludes with a call to action. "Let us embrace the spirit of innovation as a catalyst for progress and prosperity. By working together and harnessing the power of creativity and collaboration, we can build a future where innovation is not just a pathway to economic growth but a force for positive change in our lives and communities."

As the session draws to a close, the crowd is filled with a renewed sense of purpose and possibility. With innovation as their compass and collaboration as their strength, they disperse into the day, ready to embrace the challenges and opportunities of tomorrow with enthusiasm and optimism.

Kato watches them go, his heart swelling with pride. He knows that with creativity as their guide and perseverance as their ally, the residents of Ndola can pioneer a future of innovation and progress for themselves and their community.

The Role of Intellectual Property Rights

"Safeguarding Creativity: Exploring the Role of Intellectual Property Rights"

As the sun reaches its zenith over Ndola, Kato returns to the community center, ready to delve into the crucial role of intellectual property rights in fostering innovation. The atmosphere buzzes with anticipation as the residents gather once more, eager to unravel the complexities of protecting creativity and innovation.

Kato stands before the assembled crowd, his voice resonating with gravitas and importance. "Good afternoon, my friends. Today, we explore the cornerstone of innovation—the protection of intellectual property rights. Together, we shall navigate the intricate web of patents, copyrights, and trademarks that safeguard creativity and drive economic progress."

He begins with a reflective tone. "In the realm of innovation,

CHAPTER 9: INNOVATION AND TECHNOLOGICAL CHANGE

intellectual property rights serve as the bedrock upon which creativity and entrepreneurship thrive. From the inventions of Thomas Edison to the literary works of Chinua Achebe, these rights provide innovators and creators with the legal protections and incentives needed to bring their ideas to fruition. But let us not overlook the complexities of intellectual property, for within them lie the delicate balance between innovation and access, competition and exclusivity."

The crowd listens intently, their faces reflecting a mix of curiosity and concern.

"The role of intellectual property rights," Kato explains, "extends far beyond mere legal protections—it encompasses the broader societal implications of innovation, including access to knowledge, technological diffusion, and cultural diversity. From pharmaceutical patents that incentivize drug discovery to copyright laws that protect artistic expression, these rights shape the contours of our economic and cultural landscape."

He gestures to the nearby marketplace, where entrepreneurs showcase their patented inventions amidst whispers of admiration and envy. "In Ndola, we witness the importance of intellectual property rights in fostering innovation—from local artisans who rely on trademarks to protect their brands to tech startups that leverage patents to attract investment and fuel growth. These rights not only incentivize creativity and investment but also promote competition and consumer choice."

Kato then turns his attention to the challenges of intellectual property rights in a globalized world. "Beyond national borders," he explains, "lie complex issues of enforcement, harmonization, and access. In an interconnected world, where ideas flow freely across borders and digital platforms, ensuring the effective protection of intellectual property rights requires international cooperation, robust legal frameworks, and mechanisms for dispute resolution."

A concerned artist named Luka raises his hand. "But how do we strike a balance between protecting intellectual property rights and promoting access to knowledge and cultural expression? Are there any strategies for addressing the challenges of enforcement and piracy in a digital age?"

Kato's expression softens with empathy. "Ah, Luka, a pressing question indeed. Striking a balance between protection and access requires a nuanced approach that considers the diverse needs of creators, consumers, and society at large. By fostering dialogue and collaboration between stakeholders, implementing effective enforcement mechanisms, and promoting alternative models of licensing and distribution, communities can create a more inclusive and sustainable ecosystem for innovation and creativity."

He shares stories of successful initiatives that promote access to knowledge and cultural expression while respecting intellectual property rights, from open-access publishing platforms to fair-use provisions that enable transformative uses of copyrighted works. "By embracing the complexities of intellectual property rights and fostering a culture of respect and collaboration, communities can unlock the full potential of innovation and creativity for the benefit of all," Kato says, nodding to the crowd.

The audience nods in agreement, their faces reflecting a sense of understanding and determination.

Kato concludes with a call to action. "Let us embrace the importance of intellectual property rights as guardians of creativity and innovation. By working together and upholding the principles of fairness, equity, and access, we can build a future where intellectual property rights serve as instruments of progress and prosperity for all."

As the session draws to a close, the crowd is filled with a renewed sense of appreciation and responsibility. With intellectual property rights as their compass and collaboration as their strength, they disperse into the evening, ready to champion the cause of innovation and creativity in their community and beyond.

Kato watches them go, his heart swelling with pride. He knows that with respect as their guide and innovation as their ally, the residents of Ndola can build a future where creativity flourishes, knowledge thrives, and economic progress knows no bounds.

Technological Disruption and Creative Destruction

"Redefining Frontiers: Navigating Technological Disruption and Creative Destruction"

As dusk settles over Ndola, Kato returns to the community center, prepared to explore the tumultuous landscape of technological disruption and creative destruction. The air is filled with a sense of urgency and apprehension as the residents gather once more, ready to confront the challenges and opportunities presented by rapid technological change.

Kato stands before the assembled crowd, his voice carrying a tone of solemnity and resolve. "Good evening, my friends. Today, we confront a formidable force in the realm of innovation—technological disruption and creative destruction. Together, we shall navigate the turbulent waters of change and uncover the pathways to resilience and renewal."

He begins with a reflective tone. "In the evolution of economies, technological disruption and creative destruction are inevitable forces that reshape industries, redefine jobs, and transform lives. From the rise of automation to the advent of artificial intelligence, these disruptions challenge existing norms, dismantle established structures, and create both winners and losers. But let us not fear the winds of change, for within them lie the seeds of innovation, adaptation, and progress."

The crowd listens intently, their faces reflecting a mix of apprehension and determination.

"Technological disruption," Kato explains, "occurs when new technologies emerge that render existing products, services, or business models obsolete. It disrupts traditional industries, displaces workers, and reshapes consumer behaviors, often leading to upheaval and uncertainty. Similarly, creative destruction refers to the process by which outdated technologies, businesses, and practices are replaced by newer, more efficient ones, paving the way for innovation and renewal."

He gestures to the nearby marketplace, where entrepreneurs discuss the challenges of adapting to technological change amidst whispers of resilience and adaptation. "In Ndola, we witness the impact of technological disruption and creative destruction on our daily lives—from the automation of manufacturing processes to the digitization of commerce and communication. These disruptions not only pose challenges but also create opportunities for innovation, entrepreneurship, and economic renewal."

Kato then turns his attention to the importance of resilience and adaptation. "Beyond the challenges," he explains, "lie opportunities for individuals, businesses, and communities to adapt, innovate, and thrive in the face of technological disruption. By embracing lifelong learning, fostering entrepreneurial spirit, and investing in new skills and technologies, communities can build resilience and prepare for the challenges and opportunities of tomorrow."

A concerned worker named Mwaba raises her hand. "But how do we ensure that everyone can benefit from technological disruption and creative destruction? Are there any strategies for mitigating the negative impacts on vulnerable populations and fostering inclusive growth?"

Kato's expression softens with empathy. "Ah, Mwaba, a poignant question indeed. Ensuring inclusive growth in the face of technological disruption requires proactive measures that address the diverse needs of individuals and communities. By investing in education and training programs, providing support for displaced workers, and promoting policies that foster entrepreneurship and innovation, communities can create a more equitable and resilient future for all."

He shares stories of successful initiatives that empower individuals and communities to adapt and thrive in the face of technological change, from retraining programs for displaced workers to incubators that support startups in emerging industries. "By embracing the challenges of technological disruption and creative destruction with courage and determination, we can build a future where innovation serves as a force for inclusive growth and shared prosperity," Kato says, nodding to the crowd.

The audience nods in agreement, their faces reflecting a

sense of understanding and solidarity.

Kato concludes with a call to action. "Let us embrace the opportunities presented by technological disruption and creative destruction as catalysts for renewal and innovation. By working together and fostering a culture of resilience and adaptation, we can build a future where everyone has the opportunity to thrive and succeed in the face of change."

As the session draws to a close, the crowd is filled with a renewed sense of determination and hope. With resilience as their guide and innovation as their ally, they disperse into the night, ready to embrace the challenges and opportunities of technological disruption with courage and optimism.

Kato watches them go, his heart swelling with pride. He knows that with adaptability as their strength and community as their support, the residents of Ndola can navigate the turbulent waters of change and build a future of resilience and renewal for themselves and their community.

Innovation Clusters and Knowledge Spillovers

"Forging Connections: Exploring Innovation Clusters and Knowledge Spillovers"

As twilight descends over Ndola, Kato returns to the community center, ready to explore the interconnected web of innovation clusters and knowledge spillovers. The air is charged with excitement and curiosity as the residents gather once more, eager to uncover the secrets of collaborative creativity and shared discovery.

Kato stands before the assembled crowd, his voice resonating with enthusiasm and anticipation. "Good evening, my friends. Today, we embark on a journey into the heart of innovation, where clusters of creativity and knowledge spillovers drive economic growth and prosperity. Together, we shall unravel the mysteries of collaborative innovation and discover the pathways to collective success."

He begins with a contemplative reflection. "In the landscape of innovation, clusters of creativity emerge as hotbeds of collaboration, competition, and cross-pollination. From Silicon Valley to Shenzhen, these clusters bring together entrepreneurs, researchers, and investors in vibrant ecosystems where ideas flourish and innovations thrive. But let us not overlook the importance of knowledge spillovers, for within them lie the seeds of creativity, inspiration, and progress."

The crowd listens intently, their faces reflecting a mix of curiosity and excitement.

"Innovation clusters," Kato explains, "are geographic concentrations of interconnected businesses, institutions, and supporting organizations that specialize in a particular industry or field. These clusters foster collaboration, knowledge sharing, and resource pooling, creating a fertile ground for innovation and entrepreneurship to flourish. Similarly, knowledge spillovers refer to the unintended diffusion of ideas, technologies, and expertise from one entity to another, often catalyzing innovation and driving economic growth."

He gestures to the nearby marketplace, where entrepreneurs discuss the benefits of collaboration and networking amidst whispers of synergy and opportunity. "In Ndola, we witness the power of innovation clusters and knowledge spillovers in our own community—from co-working spaces and innovation hubs to research institutes and business incubators. These clusters not only promote collaboration and knowledge sharing but also foster a culture of entrepreneurship and innovation that drives economic development and prosperity."

Kato then turns his attention to the importance of connectivity and collaboration. "Beyond individual initiatives," he explains, "lie opportunities for communities to create ecosystems that support innovation and entrepreneurship. By investing in infrastructure, fostering partnerships between industry and academia, and promoting a culture of openness and collaboration, communities can harness the power of innovation clusters and knowledge spillovers to drive economic growth and prosperity."

A budding entrepreneur named Chanda raises her hand. "But how do we foster innovation clusters and promote knowledge spillovers in our community? Are there any strategies for creating a conducive environment for collaboration and creativity?"

Kato's expression brightens with enthusiasm. "Ah, Chanda, an excellent question indeed. Fostering innovation clusters and promoting knowledge spillovers requires a multifaceted approach that engages stakeholders from across sectors and disciplines. By creating networking opportunities, providing access to resources and expertise, and offering support for collaborative projects and ventures, communities can create an environment where innovation thrives and prosperity abounds."

He shares stories of successful initiatives that have catalyzed innovation clusters and facilitated knowledge spillovers in diverse settings, from public-private partnerships that support research and development to community-driven initiatives that promote entrepreneurship and creativity. "By embracing the power of collaboration and connectivity, we can unlock the full potential of innovation clusters and knowledge spillovers to drive economic growth, create jobs, and improve lives," Kato says, nodding to the crowd.

The audience nods in agreement, their faces reflecting a sense of understanding and determination.

Kato concludes with a call to action. "Let us embrace the spirit of collaboration and connectivity as catalysts for innovation and prosperity. By working together and fostering a culture of openness, creativity, and collaboration, we can build a future where innovation clusters thrive, knowledge spillovers abound, and economic prosperity is shared by all."

As the session draws to a close, the crowd is filled with a renewed sense of excitement and possibility. With collaboration as their guide and creativity as their strength, they disperse into the night, ready to embrace the opportunities of innovation clusters and knowledge spillovers with enthusiasm and optimism.

Kato watches them go, his heart swelling with pride. He knows that with collaboration as their compass and community as their support, the residents of Ndola can build a future of prosperity and progress for themselves and their community.

Technological Unemployment and Job Polarization

"Navigating Change: Confronting Technological Unemployment and Job Polarization"

As the sun reaches its zenith over Ndola, Kato returns to the community center, prepared to confront the challenges posed by technological unemployment and job polarization. The air is thick with a sense of urgency and concern as the residents gather once more, ready to explore the complex dynamics of technological change and its impact on the workforce.

Kato stands before the assembled crowd, his voice carrying a tone of empathy and determination. "Good afternoon, my friends. Today, we confront a pressing issue in the realm of innovation—technological unemployment and job polarization. Together, we shall navigate the shifting landscape of work and employment and explore strategies for building resilience and adaptation in the face of change."

He begins with a sobering reflection. "In the wake of technological advancements, the nature of work is undergoing profound transformation. Automation, artificial intelligence, and robotics are reshaping industries, disrupting traditional job roles, and creating both opportunities and challenges for workers. But let us not succumb to fear and uncertainty, for within them lie opportunities for innovation, retraining, and renewal."

The crowd listens intently, their faces reflecting a mix of concern and determination.

"Technological unemployment," Kato explains, "refers to the displacement of workers by machines and automation, as tasks that were once performed by humans are now automated by technology. This phenomenon poses challenges for workers who may find themselves without the skills or opportunities needed to adapt to the changing labor market. Similarly, job polarization refers to the widening gap between high-skill, high-wage jobs and low-skill, low-wage jobs, with fewer opportunities available in the middle."

He gestures to the nearby marketplace, where workers discuss the challenges of adapting to technological change amidst whispers of uncertainty and insecurity. "In Ndola, we witness the impact of technological unemployment and job polarization on our own community—from the automation of manufacturing processes to the digitization of services and administration. These changes not only pose challenges for workers but also create opportunities for innovation, entrepreneurship, and economic diversification."

Kato then turns his attention to the importance of adaptation and resilience. "Beyond the challenges," he explains, "lie opportunities for workers to adapt, retrain, and reskill in order to thrive in the changing labor market. By investing in lifelong learning, fostering a culture of innovation, and providing support for displaced workers, communities can build resilience and prepare for the challenges and opportunities of tomorrow."

A concerned worker named Mwaba raises her hand. "But how do we ensure that everyone can benefit from technological change and automation? Are there any strategies for promoting inclusive growth and shared prosperity in the face of technological unemployment and job polarization?"

Kato's expression softens with empathy. "Ah, Mwaba, an important question indeed. Promoting inclusive growth in the face of technological change requires a concerted effort to address the diverse needs of workers and communities. By investing in education and training programs that equip workers with the skills needed for the jobs of the future, providing support for displaced workers to transition to new industries and occupations, and implementing policies that promote fair wages, job security, and social protection, communities can create a more equitable and resilient future for all."

He shares stories of successful initiatives that have helped workers adapt and thrive in the face of technological change, from government-sponsored training programs to community-driven initiatives that support entrepreneurship and economic diversification. "By embracing the challenges of technological unemployment and job polarization with courage and determination, we can build a future where innovation serves as a force for inclusive growth and shared prosperity," Kato says, nodding to the crowd.

The audience nods in agreement, their faces reflecting a sense of understanding and solidarity.

Kato concludes with a call to action. "Let us embrace the opportunities presented by technological change as catalysts for renewal and adaptation. By working together and fostering a culture of resilience and innovation, we can build a future where everyone has the opportunity to thrive and succeed in the face of change."

As the session draws to a close, the crowd is filled with a renewed sense of determination and hope. With adaptation as their guide and resilience as their strength, they disperse into the evening, ready to embrace the challenges and opportunities of technological change with courage and optimism.

Kato watches them go, his heart swelling with pride. He knows that with compassion as their compass and community as their support, the residents of Ndola can navigate the shifting landscape of work and employment and build a future of prosperity and progress for themselves and their community.

Policies to Foster Innovation and Entrepreneurship

"Forging Futures: Crafting Policies to Foster Innovation and Entrepreneurship"

As evening falls over Ndola, Kato returns to the community center, prepared to discuss the crucial role of policies in fostering innovation and entrepreneurship. The atmosphere crackles with anticipation as the residents gather once more, eager to explore strategies for driving economic growth and prosperity.

Kato stands before the assembled crowd, his voice infused with determination and purpose. "Good evening, my friends. Today, we delve into the realm of policy—exploring the levers of change that can ignite the flames of innovation and entrepreneurship. Together, we shall chart a course towards a future of opportunity, creativity, and prosperity."

He begins with a resolute tone. "In the journey of economic development, policies play a pivotal role in shaping the conditions for innovation and entrepreneurship to thrive. From regulatory frameworks to investment incentives, these policies create the environment in which businesses can flourish, ideas can blossom, and communities can prosper. But let us not underestimate the complexity of policymaking, for within it lies the power to unlock human potential and drive transformative change."

The crowd listens intently, their faces reflecting a mix of

eagerness and determination.

"Policies to foster innovation and entrepreneurship," Kato explains, "encompass a wide range of initiatives aimed at supporting research and development, facilitating access to finance, promoting industry-academic collaboration, and fostering a culture of entrepreneurship. These policies not only provide the necessary resources and incentives for innovation but also create a supportive environment where entrepreneurs can turn their ideas into reality."

He gestures to the nearby marketplace, where entrepreneurs discuss the impact of government initiatives amidst whispers of optimism and opportunity. "In Ndola, we witness the impact of policies to foster innovation and entrepreneurship on our own community—from tax incentives for research and development to business incubation programs that support startups and small businesses. These policies not only stimulate economic growth and job creation but also empower individuals and communities to realize their full potential."

Kato then turns his attention to the importance of collaboration and inclusivity in policymaking. "Beyond individual initiatives," he explains, "lie opportunities for communities to engage stakeholders from across sectors and disciplines in the policymaking process. By fostering dialogue, soliciting feedback, and incorporating diverse perspectives, communities can ensure that policies are responsive to the needs and aspirations of all citizens."

A young entrepreneur named Chanda raises her hand. "But how do we ensure that policies to foster innovation and entrepreneurship are inclusive and equitable? Are there any strategies for addressing the needs of marginalized communities and promoting social inclusion?"

Kato's expression softens with empathy. "Ah, Chanda, a crucial question indeed. Ensuring inclusivity and equity in policymaking requires a commitment to social justice, fairness, and empowerment. By implementing targeted programs and initiatives that address the needs of marginalized communities, promoting diversity and inclusion in entrepreneurship ecosystems, and providing support for underrepresented groups, communities can create an environment where everyone has the opportunity to participate and succeed."

He shares stories of successful initiatives that have empowered marginalized communities and promoted social inclusion, from microfinance programs that support women entrepreneurs to mentorship networks for minority-owned businesses. "By embracing the principles of inclusivity and equity in policymaking, we can build a future where innovation and entrepreneurship serve as engines of social mobility and shared prosperity," Kato says, nodding to the crowd.

The audience nods in agreement, their faces reflecting a sense of understanding and solidarity.

Kato concludes with a call to action. "Let us embrace the power of policy as a catalyst for change and transformation. By working together and fostering a culture of collaboration, inclusivity, and innovation, we can build a future where everyone has the opportunity to thrive and succeed."

As the session draws to a close, the crowd is filled with a renewed sense of purpose and determination. With policy as their compass and collaboration as their strength, they disperse into the night, ready to embrace the opportunities of innovation and entrepreneurship with courage and optimism.

Kato watches them go, his heart swelling with pride. He

knows that with determination as their guide and community as their support, the residents of Ndola can craft a future of opportunity, creativity, and prosperity for themselves and their community.

10

Chapter 10: Environmental Economics

The Economics of Natural Resources

"Guardians of the Earth: Unveiling the Economics of Natural Resources"

Under the midday sun in Ndola, Kato returns to the community center, prepared to delve into the intricate world of environmental economics. The air is filled with a sense of reverence and concern as the residents gather once more, ready to explore the delicate balance between economic growth and environmental stewardship.

Kato stands before the assembled crowd, his voice echoing with reverence and determination. "Good afternoon, my friends. Today, we embark on a journey into the heart of environmental economics, where the fate of our planet intersects with the imperatives of economic progress. Together, we shall uncover the complexities of natural resource management and chart a course towards sustainability and resilience."

He begins with a reflective tone. "In the tapestry of economic activity, natural resources serve as the lifeblood of our planet—sustaining ecosystems, fueling industries, and providing livelihoods for countless communities. From forests to fisheries, these resources are not only sources of wealth and prosperity but also pillars of biodiversity and ecological integrity. But let us not forget the fragility of nature, for within it lies the need for careful stewardship and responsible management."

The crowd listens intently, their faces reflecting a mix of reverence and concern.

"The economics of natural resources," Kato explains, "encompasses the principles and practices of resource allocation, extraction, and conservation within the framework of economic decision-making. It explores the ways in which markets, policies, and human behavior shape the exploitation and preservation of natural assets, from minerals and fossil fuels to water and wildlife."

He gestures to the nearby marketplace, where vendors discuss the importance of sustainable practices amidst whispers of reverence and awe. "In Ndola, we witness the impact of natural resource economics on our own community—from mining operations that drive economic growth to conservation efforts that protect biodiversity and ecosystem services. These dynamics not only shape the landscape of economic activity but also influence the health and well-being of present and future generations."

Kato then turns his attention to the importance of sustainability and stewardship. "Beyond the imperatives of economic growth," he explains, "lie the principles of sustainability and resilience that guide responsible resource management. By embracing practices that promote conservation, reduce waste, and mitigate environmental degradation, communities can safeguard natural resources for future generations and ensure the long-term viability of their economies."

A concerned environmentalist named Luka raises his hand. "But how do we reconcile the demands of economic development with the imperatives of environmental conservation? Are there any strategies for promoting sustainable resource management and mitigating the impacts of resource depletion and pollution?"

Kato's expression softens with empathy. "Ah, Luka, a profound question indeed. Reconciling economic development with environmental conservation requires a holistic approach that integrates the principles of sustainability into all aspects of decision-making. By implementing policies that internalize environmental costs, promote renewable energy and resource efficiency, and incentivize sustainable practices, communities can achieve a harmonious balance between economic prosperity and ecological integrity."

He shares stories of successful initiatives that have promoted sustainable resource management and conservation, from renewable energy projects that reduce greenhouse gas emissions to reforestation programs that restore degraded landscapes. "By embracing the principles of environmental economics and stewardship, we can build a future where economic progress coexists with environmental sustainability," Kato says, nodding to the crowd.

The audience nods in agreement, their faces reflecting a sense of understanding and commitment.

Kato concludes with a call to action. "Let us embrace the role of stewards of the Earth, tasked with safeguarding natural resources for future generations. By working together and fostering a culture of sustainability and resilience, we can build a future where economic prosperity thrives in harmony with ecological integrity."

As the session draws to a close, the crowd is filled with a renewed sense of purpose and determination. With stewardship as their guide and sustainability as their strength, they disperse into the afternoon, ready to embrace the challenges and opportunities of environmental economics with courage and conviction.

Kato watches them go, his heart swelling with pride. He knows that with reverence as their compass and community as their support, the residents of Ndola can build a future where the Earth thrives, and prosperity is shared by all.

Externalities and Environmental Degradation

"Balancing Acts: Confronting Externalities and Environmental Degradation"

As dusk settles over Ndola, Kato returns to the community center, prepared to confront the pressing issues of externalities and environmental degradation within the realm of environmental economics. The atmosphere is tinged with a sense of urgency and responsibility as the residents gather once more, ready to delve into the complexities of human impact on the environment.

Kato stands before the assembled crowd, his voice resonating with concern and resolve. "Good evening, my friends.

CHAPTER 10: ENVIRONMENTAL ECONOMICS

Today, we confront a formidable challenge in the realm of environmental economics—externalities and their profound impact on our planet's health and well-being. Together, we shall unravel the complexities of human activity and its unintended consequences, and explore strategies for mitigating environmental degradation and promoting sustainability."

He begins with a somber reflection. "In the pursuit of economic progress, human activities often give rise to externalities—unintended side effects that affect third parties, often with negative consequences for the environment and society at large. From pollution to deforestation, these externalities pose threats to ecological balance, human health, and future generations. But let us not despair, for within the challenges lie opportunities for innovation, regulation, and collective action."

The crowd listens intently, their faces reflecting a mix of concern and determination.

"Externalities and environmental degradation," Kato explains, "manifest in various forms, from air and water pollution to habitat destruction and climate change. These phenomena result from market failures and policy shortcomings that fail to internalize the true costs of production and consumption, leading to overexploitation of natural resources and degradation of ecosystems."

He gestures to the nearby marketplace, where vendors discuss the need for responsible practices amidst whispers of urgency and responsibility. "In Ndola, we witness the consequences of externalities and environmental degradation on our own community—from industrial pollution that contaminates waterways to land degradation that threatens agricultural productivity. These challenges not only jeopardize the health and well-being of present and future generations but also undermine the sustainability of our economies and societies."

Kato then turns his attention to the importance of accountability and regulation. "Beyond the consequences," he explains, "lie opportunities for communities to address externalities and promote environmental stewardship through regulation, incentives, and collective action. By implementing policies that internalize environmental costs, promote sustainable practices, and hold polluters accountable, communities can mitigate the impacts of externalities and safeguard the health and well-being of both people and planet."

A concerned citizen named Sarah raises her hand. "But how do we ensure that policies to address externalities are effective and equitable? Are there any strategies for engaging stakeholders and fostering collective action in support of environmental conservation and sustainability?"

Kato's expression softens with empathy. "Ah, Sarah, a vital question indeed. Ensuring the effectiveness and equity of policies to address externalities requires a participatory approach that engages stakeholders from all sectors of society. By fostering dialogue, soliciting feedback, and building consensus around shared goals and values, communities can create a sense of ownership and responsibility for environmental conservation and sustainability."

He shares stories of successful initiatives that have mobilized communities to address environmental challenges, from grassroots movements that advocate for clean air and water to public-private partnerships that promote sustainable land management and conservation. "By embracing the principles of environmental economics and collective action," Kato says, nodding to the crowd, "we can build a future where economic prosperity thrives in harmony with environmental sustainability."

The audience nods in agreement, their faces reflecting a sense of understanding and determination.

Kato concludes with a call to action. "Let us embrace our responsibility as stewards of the Earth, tasked with safeguarding the environment for present and future generations. By working together and fostering a culture of accountability and sustainability, we can build a future where prosperity and well-being are shared by all."

As the session draws to a close, the crowd is filled with a renewed sense of purpose and commitment. With accountability as their guide and collective action as their strength, they disperse into the night, ready to confront the challenges of externalities and environmental degradation with courage and conviction.

Kato watches them go, his heart swelling with pride. He knows that with determination as their compass and community as their support, the residents of Ndola can build a future where the Earth thrives, and prosperity is shared by all.

Valuation of Ecosystem Services

"Nature's Worth: Unveiling the Valuation of Ecosystem Services"

Under the starry night sky in Ndola, Kato returns to the community center, ready to explore the intricate concept of valuing ecosystem services within the realm of environmental economics. The atmosphere is filled with a sense of wonder and curiosity as the residents gather once more, eager to unravel the hidden treasures of nature's contributions to human well-being.

Kato stands before the assembled crowd, his voice carrying a tone of reverence and inquiry. "Good evening, my friends. Today, we embark on a journey into the heart of environmental economics—exploring the invaluable services provided by nature and the challenges of assigning them a monetary value. Together, we shall uncover the hidden riches of ecosystems and discover the pathways to preserving their integrity and vitality."

He begins with a contemplative reflection. "In the intricate web of life, ecosystems provide a myriad of services that sustain human societies and enhance our quality of life. From clean air and water to pollination and climate regulation, these services are essential for our survival and well-being. But let us not overlook the complexities of valuing these services, for within them lie the keys to unlocking nature's true worth."

The crowd listens intently, their faces reflecting a mix of curiosity and awe.

"The valuation of ecosystem services," Kato explains, "encompasses the processes of quantifying and assigning a monetary value to the benefits provided by nature to human societies. It seeks to capture the full range of contributions that ecosystems make to our well-being, from tangible goods such as food and timber to intangible benefits such as cultural and recreational values."

He gestures to the nearby marketplace, where vendors discuss the importance of preserving natural resources amidst whispers of appreciation and respect. "In Ndola, we witness the profound impacts of ecosystem services on our own community—from the fertile soils that sustain agriculture to the lush forests that provide habitat for wildlife and recreational opportunities for residents. These services not only enhance our quality of life but also underpin the sustainability of our economies and societies."

Kato then turns his attention to the challenges of valuation. "Beyond the benefits," he explains, "lie the challenges of assigning a monetary value to ecosystem services, which are often undervalued or overlooked in traditional economic assessments. Factors such as market failures, information asymmetries, and ethical considerations complicate the process of valuation, making it difficult to fully capture the true worth of nature's contributions."

A concerned conservationist named Mwaba raises her hand. "But how do we overcome the challenges of valuing ecosystem services? Are there any strategies for integrating these values into decision-making processes and promoting sustainable resource management?"

Kato's expression softens with empathy. "Ah, Mwaba, an important question indeed. Overcoming the challenges of valuing ecosystem services requires a multi-faceted approach that integrates economic, ecological, and social considerations into decision-making processes. By employing methods such as cost-benefit analysis, ecosystem accounting, and participatory valuation techniques, communities can gain a more comprehensive understanding of the value of nature's contributions and incorporate these values into policy and planning."

He shares stories of successful initiatives that have integrated ecosystem service valuation into decision-making processes, from watershed management programs that recognize the value of clean water to ecotourism projects that promote the preservation of biodiversity and cultural heritage. "By embracing the principles of ecosystem service valuation," Kato says, nodding to the crowd, "we can build a future where economic prosperity thrives in harmony with ecological integrity."

The audience nods in agreement, their faces reflecting a sense of understanding and appreciation.

Kato concludes with a call to action. "Let us recognize the invaluable contributions of nature to our well-being and prosperity. By working together and fostering a culture of stewardship and sustainability, we can build a future where ecosystems thrive, and prosperity is shared by all."

As the session draws to a close, the crowd is filled with a renewed sense of appreciation and commitment. With stewardship as their guide and sustainability as their strength, they disperse into the night, ready to embrace the challenges of valuing ecosystem services with courage and conviction.

Kato watches them go, his heart swelling with pride. He knows that with determination as their compass and community as their support, the residents of Ndola can build a future where the Earth thrives, and prosperity is shared by all.

Market-Based Instruments for Environmental Protection

"Harmony in Exchange: Exploring Market-Based Instruments for Environmental Protection"

As dawn breaks over Ndola, Kato returns to the community center, prepared to unravel the complexities of market-based instruments for environmental protection within the realm of environmental economics. The atmosphere is alive with anticipation and curiosity as the residents gather once more, eager to explore innovative solutions to safeguarding the environment.

Kato stands before the assembled crowd, his voice carrying a tone of optimism and inquiry. "Good morning, my friends. Today, we embark on a journey into the realm of environmental economics—unraveling the potential of market-based instruments to foster environmental protection and conservation. Together, we shall explore the power of markets as tools for promoting sustainability and stewardship."

He begins with a contemplative reflection. "In the marketplace of ideas, market-based instruments offer innovative solutions to the challenges of environmental protection. From emissions trading to pollution taxes, these instruments harness the power of economic incentives to align private interests with public goods. But let us not overlook the complexities of market dynamics, for within them lie opportunities for innovation, collaboration, and transformation."

The crowd listens intently, their faces reflecting a mix of curiosity and determination.

"Market-based instruments for environmental protection,"

Kato explains, "leverage the principles of supply and demand to internalize the costs of environmental degradation and incentivize conservation and sustainable practices. By creating economic incentives for pollution reduction, resource conservation, and ecosystem restoration, these instruments promote efficiency, innovation, and accountability in the pursuit of environmental goals."

He gestures to the nearby marketplace, where vendors discuss the benefits of market-based approaches amidst whispers of excitement and anticipation. "In Ndola, we witness the potential of market-based instruments to drive environmental progress—from carbon markets that incentivize emissions reductions to payments for ecosystem services that reward conservation efforts. These instruments not only provide economic opportunities for businesses and communities but also contribute to the preservation of nature's wealth and resilience."

Kato then turns his attention to the diversity of market-based approaches. "Beyond the solutions," he explains, "lie a multitude of market-based instruments that can be tailored to address specific environmental challenges and contexts. From cap-and-trade systems to green bonds, these instruments offer flexibility and scalability in achieving environmental objectives, empowering communities and businesses to innovate and collaborate in the pursuit of sustainability."

A curious entrepreneur named Chanda raises her hand. "But how do we ensure that market-based instruments are effective and equitable? Are there any strategies for maximizing their benefits while minimizing their potential drawbacks?"

Kato's expression softens with empathy. "Ah, Chanda, an insightful question indeed. Ensuring the effectiveness and equity of market-based instruments requires careful design, implementation, and monitoring. By incorporating principles of transparency, accountability, and stakeholder engagement into their design, communities can ensure that these instruments are responsive to the needs and aspirations of all citizens."

He shares stories of successful initiatives that have harnessed the power of market-based instruments to promote environmental protection and sustainability, from emissions trading schemes that reduce greenhouse gas emissions to payments for ecosystem services programs that conserve biodiversity and enhance livelihoods. "By embracing the principles of environmental economics and market-based solutions," Kato says, nodding to the crowd, "we can build a future where economic prosperity thrives in harmony with environmental sustainability."

The audience nods in agreement, their faces reflecting a sense of understanding and determination.

Kato concludes with a call to action. "Let us harness the power of markets as tools for environmental protection and conservation. By working together and fostering a culture of innovation, collaboration, and accountability, we can build a future where prosperity and sustainability go hand in hand."

As the session draws to a close, the crowd is filled with a renewed sense of optimism and commitment. With innovation as their guide and collaboration as their strength, they disperse into the morning, ready to embrace the challenges and opportunities of market-based instruments for environmental protection with courage and conviction.

Kato watches them go, his heart swelling with pride. He knows that with determination as their compass and community as their support, the residents of Ndola can build a future where the Earth thrives, and prosperity is shared by all.

Climate Change Economics and Policy Responses

"Navigating the Climate: Charting Economics and Policy Responses to Climate Change"

As twilight descends upon Ndola, Kato returns to the community center, ready to delve into the intricate realm of climate change economics and policy responses within the realm of environmental economics. The atmosphere is charged with a sense of urgency and determination as the residents gather once more, eager to confront one of the greatest challenges of our time.

Kato stands before the assembled crowd, his voice echoing with solemnity and resolve. "Good evening, my friends. Today, we confront a formidable challenge that transcends borders and generations—climate change and its profound impacts on our planet's health and well-being. Together, we shall explore the economics of climate change and chart a course towards resilience, adaptation, and mitigation."

He begins with a somber reflection. "In the unfolding saga of climate change, the stakes could not be higher. Rising temperatures, changing weather patterns, and extreme events threaten ecosystems, livelihoods, and the very fabric of human societies. But let us not succumb to despair, for within the challenges lie opportunities for innovation, collaboration, and transformation."

The crowd listens intently, their faces reflecting a mix of concern and determination.

"Climate change economics," Kato explains, "encompasses the principles and practices of understanding, quantifying, and addressing the economic impacts of climate change. From the costs of adaptation and mitigation to the benefits of transitioning to a low-carbon economy, these dynamics shape the choices and actions of individuals, businesses, and governments in response to the climate crisis."

He gestures to the nearby marketplace, where vendors discuss the imperative of climate action amidst whispers of urgency and solidarity. "In Ndola, we witness the impacts of climate change on our own community—from changing rainfall patterns that affect agriculture to increased frequency of extreme weather events that threaten infrastructure and livelihoods. These challenges not only demand immediate action but also underscore the importance of global cooperation and solidarity in confronting the climate crisis."

Kato then turns his attention to the importance of policy responses. "Beyond the impacts," he explains, "lie the policy responses that are essential for addressing the root causes of climate change and building resilience to its impacts. From international agreements such as the Paris Agreement to national policies such as carbon pricing and renewable energy incentives, these responses provide the framework and incentives for transitioning to a low-carbon, climate-resilient future."

A concerned youth activist named Chipo raises her hand. "But how do we ensure that policy responses to climate change are ambitious, equitable, and effective? Are there any strategies for mobilizing public support and political will for climate action?"

Kato's expression softens with empathy. "Ah, Chipo, a

critical question indeed. Ensuring ambitious and equitable policy responses to climate change requires leadership, collaboration, and engagement across all sectors of society. By raising awareness, mobilizing public support, and holding governments and businesses accountable for their actions, communities can drive meaningful change and push for policies that prioritize environmental sustainability and social justice."

He shares stories of successful initiatives that have mobilized communities to take action on climate change, from youth-led protests demanding climate action to grassroots campaigns advocating for renewable energy and sustainable land use practices. "By embracing the principles of climate change economics and policy responses," Kato says, nodding to the crowd, "we can build a future where economic prosperity thrives in harmony with environmental sustainability."

The audience nods in agreement, their faces reflecting a sense of understanding and determination.

Kato concludes with a call to action. "Let us rise to the challenge of climate change with courage and conviction. By working together and fostering a culture of resilience, adaptation, and mitigation, we can build a future where humanity thrives in harmony with nature."

As the session draws to a close, the crowd is filled with a renewed sense of purpose and commitment. With solidarity as their guide and determination as their strength, they disperse into the night, ready to confront the climate crisis with courage and conviction.

Kato watches them go, his heart swelling with pride. He knows that with determination as their compass and community as their support, the residents of Ndola can build a future where the Earth thrives, and prosperity is shared by all.

Sustainable Development Strategies

"Pathways to Prosperity: Embracing Sustainable Development Strategies"

As the sun rises over Ndola, Kato returns to the community center, prepared to explore sustainable development strategies within the realm of environmental economics. The air is charged with anticipation and hope as the residents gather once more, eager to uncover pathways to a future where prosperity and sustainability go hand in hand.

Kato stands before the assembled crowd, his voice resonating with optimism and determination. "Good morning, my friends. Today, we embark on a journey into the realm of sustainable development—exploring strategies to build a future where economic prosperity thrives in harmony with environmental sustainability. Together, we shall explore the principles and practices that guide us towards a more resilient and equitable world."

He begins with a reflective tone. "In the pursuit of progress, sustainable development offers a vision of prosperity that transcends mere economic growth. It seeks to balance the imperatives of economic prosperity, social inclusion, and environmental stewardship, ensuring that present needs are met without compromising the ability of future generations to meet their own needs."

The crowd listens intently, their faces reflecting a mix of curiosity and determination.

"Sustainable development strategies," Kato explains,

"encompass a wide range of approaches that integrate economic, social, and environmental considerations into decision-making processes. From green infrastructure investments to sustainable agriculture practices, these strategies aim to promote resilience, inclusivity, and long-term prosperity."

He gestures to the nearby marketplace, where vendors discuss the importance of sustainability amidst whispers of enthusiasm and collaboration. "In Ndola, we witness the potential of sustainable development strategies to transform our community—from renewable energy projects that provide clean and affordable power to inclusive business models that create opportunities for marginalized groups. These strategies not only drive economic growth but also foster social cohesion and environmental stewardship."

Kato then turns his attention to the importance of collaboration and innovation. "Beyond the solutions," he explains, "lie the opportunities for collaboration and innovation that are essential for advancing sustainable development. By forging partnerships between governments, businesses, and civil society, communities can leverage resources, expertise, and creativity to address complex challenges and seize opportunities for positive change."

A concerned community leader named Tendai raises her hand. "But how do we ensure that sustainable development strategies are inclusive and equitable? Are there any principles or frameworks that can guide us in promoting social justice and empowerment?"

Kato's expression softens with empathy. "Ah, Tendai, an important question indeed. Ensuring inclusive and equitable sustainable development requires a commitment to principles such as social justice, human rights, and gender equality. By prioritizing the needs and voices of marginalized communities, promoting access to education, healthcare, and economic opportunities, and fostering participatory decision-making processes, communities can create an environment where everyone has the opportunity to thrive."

He shares stories of successful initiatives that have embraced sustainable development principles to promote social inclusion and empowerment, from microfinance programs that empower women entrepreneurs to community-led conservation efforts that protect biodiversity and livelihoods. "By embracing the principles of sustainable development," Kato says, nodding to the crowd, "we can build a future where prosperity is shared by all."

The audience nods in agreement, their faces reflecting a sense of understanding and determination.

Kato concludes with a call to action. "Let us embrace the principles of sustainable development as our guiding compass. By working together and fostering a culture of collaboration, innovation, and inclusivity, we can build a future where economic prosperity thrives in harmony with environmental sustainability and social justice."

As the session draws to a close, the crowd is filled with a renewed sense of hope and determination. With sustainable development as their guide and community as their support, they disperse into the morning, ready to embrace the challenges and opportunities of building a better future for themselves and generations to come.

Kato watches them go, his heart swelling with pride. He knows that with determination as their compass and collaboration as their strength, the residents of Ndola can build a future where prosperity, sustainability, and social justice are woven into the fabric of everyday life.

11

Chapter 11: Urban and Regional Economics

Theories of Urban Agglomeration

"City Lights: Unraveling Theories of Urban Agglomeration"

In the heart of Ndola, amidst the bustling streets and vibrant markets, Kato returns to the community center, ready to explore the intricate theories of urban agglomeration within the realm of urban and regional economics. The air is alive with energy and curiosity as the residents gather once more, eager to unravel the mysteries of city life.

Kato stands before the assembled crowd, his voice filled with enthusiasm and intrigue. "Good evening, my friends. Today, we embark on a journey into the realm of urban and regional economics—exploring the theories of urban agglomeration and the dynamics that shape the growth and development of cities. Together, we shall delve into the vibrant tapestry of urban life and uncover the forces that drive economic prosperity and innovation."

He begins with a reflective tone. "In the mosaic of human civilization, cities stand as beacons of progress and opportunity. They are vibrant hubs of economic activity, cultural exchange, and social interaction, where people come together to live, work, and play. But let us not overlook the complexities of urban agglomeration, for within them lie the keys to understanding the dynamics of urban growth and development."

The crowd listens intently, their faces reflecting a mix of curiosity and anticipation.

"Theories of urban agglomeration," Kato explains, "seek to unravel the mysteries of why cities exist, how they grow, and what makes them thrive. From the pioneering insights of urban economists such as Alfred Marshall and Jane Jacobs to contemporary theories of agglomeration economies and network effects, these theories offer a lens through which to understand the spatial organization of economic activity and the clustering of firms and industries in urban areas."

He gestures to the nearby marketplace, where vendors discuss the benefits of clustering amidst whispers of excitement and collaboration. "In Ndola, we witness the dynamics of urban agglomeration in action—from the clustering of businesses in commercial districts to the concentration of skilled workers and knowledge-intensive industries in urban centers. These dynamics not only drive economic growth and innovation but also shape the social and spatial fabric of our communities."

Kato then turns his attention to the importance of understanding urban dynamics. "Beyond the theories," he explains, "lie the implications for urban planning, policy, and governance. By understanding the forces that shape urban agglomeration, communities can make informed decisions about infrastructure investment, land use regulation, and economic development strategies that promote sustainable growth, inclusive prosperity, and vibrant, livable cities."

A curious urban planner named Chisala raises her hand. "But how do we ensure that urban development is inclusive and sustainable? Are there any strategies for promoting equitable access to opportunities and resources in cities?"

Kato's expression softens with empathy. "Ah, Chisala, a crucial question indeed. Ensuring inclusive and sustainable urban development requires a commitment to principles such as social equity, environmental sustainability, and participatory governance. By prioritizing investments in affordable housing, public transportation, green spaces, and social services, communities can create cities that are accessible, resilient, and vibrant for all residents."

He shares stories of successful initiatives that have embraced inclusive and sustainable urban development principles, from mixed-income housing projects that promote social integration to urban revitalization efforts that reclaim vacant lots for community gardens and public parks. "By embracing the theories of urban agglomeration," Kato says, nodding to the crowd, "we can build cities that are not only engines of economic growth and innovation but also beacons of social inclusion and environmental stewardship."

The audience nods in agreement, their faces reflecting a sense of understanding and determination.

Kato concludes with a call to action. "Let us embrace the theories of urban agglomeration as our guide to building cities of the future. By working together and fostering a culture of collaboration, innovation, and inclusivity, we can create urban spaces that are vibrant, resilient, and equitable for all."

As the session draws to a close, the crowd is filled with a renewed sense of hope and determination. With urban agglomeration as their guide and community as their support, they disperse into the night, ready to embrace the challenges and opportunities of building cities that are truly worthy of their residents' dreams and aspirations.

Kato watches them go, his heart swelling with pride. He knows that with determination as their compass and collaboration as their strength, the residents of Ndola can build cities that are not only prosperous and innovative but also inclusive and sustainable for generations to come.

Urbanization Trends and Challenges

"City Horizons: Navigating Urbanization Trends and Challenges"

As the sun sets over Ndola, Kato returns to the community center, prepared to delve into the complexities of urbanization trends and challenges within the realm of urban and regional economics. The atmosphere crackles with anticipation and concern as the residents gather once more, eager to navigate the path towards sustainable urban development.

Kato stands before the assembled crowd, his voice resonating with empathy and determination. "Good evening, my friends. Today, we confront the ever-evolving landscape of urbanization—exploring the trends and challenges that shape the growth and development of cities. Together, we shall unravel the complexities of urban life and chart a course towards inclusive, resilient, and sustainable urban futures."

He begins with a reflective tone. "In the unfolding tapestry of human history, urbanization stands as a defining phenomenon of our time. From the rise of megacities to the proliferation of informal settlements, cities have become the epicenters of human civilization, where dreams are pursued and challenges are confronted. But let us not overlook the complexities of urbanization, for within them lie both opportunities and challenges that demand our attention and action."

The crowd listens intently, their faces reflecting a mix of curiosity and concern.

"Urbanization trends," Kato explains, "are characterized by rapid population growth, spatial expansion, and social transformation. From the rural-to-urban migration to the demographic shifts driven by globalization and technological change, these trends shape the spatial, social, and economic dynamics of cities, presenting both opportunities for prosperity and challenges for sustainability."

He gestures to the nearby marketplace, where vendors discuss the impacts of urbanization amidst whispers of uncertainty and resilience. "In Ndola, we witness the effects of urbanization on our own community—from the expansion of informal settlements to the strain on infrastructure and services. These challenges not only demand innovative solutions but also underscore the importance of planning, governance, and community engagement in shaping the future of our cities."

Kato then turns his attention to the importance of addressing urban challenges. "Beyond the trends," he explains, "lie the challenges that accompany rapid urbanization, from inadequate housing and infrastructure to social inequality and environmental degradation. By understanding and addressing these challenges, communities can unlock the full potential of urbanization as a driver of inclusive growth, social cohesion, and environmental sustainability."

A concerned community organizer named Mulenga raises her hand. "But how do we address the challenges of urbanization in a way that is equitable and sustainable? Are there any strategies for promoting inclusive urban development and resilience?"

Kato's expression softens with empathy. "Ah, Mulenga, a crucial question indeed. Addressing the challenges of urbanization requires a multi-faceted approach that integrates social equity, environmental sustainability, and economic resilience into urban planning and governance. By prioritizing investments in affordable housing, public transportation, green spaces, and social services, communities can create cities that are inclusive, livable, and resilient for all residents."

He shares stories of successful initiatives that have embraced inclusive and sustainable urban development principles, from participatory slum upgrading projects that empower residents to community-led infrastructure improvements that enhance resilience to climate change. "By embracing the challenges of urbanization," Kato says, nodding to the crowd, "we can build cities that are not only vibrant and prosperous but also inclusive and sustainable for generations to come."

The audience nods in agreement, their faces reflecting a sense of understanding and determination.

Kato concludes with a call to action. "Let us embrace the challenges of urbanization as opportunities for positive change. By working together and fostering a culture of collaboration, innovation, and resilience, we can build cities that are worthy of our aspirations and reflective of our values."

As the session draws to a close, the crowd is filled with a renewed sense of hope and determination. With urbanization as their guide and community as their support, they disperse into the night, ready to confront the challenges and opportunities of building cities that are truly worthy of their residents' dreams and aspirations.

Kato watches them go, his heart swelling with pride. He knows that with determination as their compass and collaboration as their strength, the residents of Ndola can build cities that are not only prosperous and innovative but also inclusive and sustainable for generations to come.

Economic Geography and Spatial Inequality

"Map of Progress: Navigating Economic Geography and Spatial Inequality"

As dawn breaks over Ndola, Kato returns to the community center, ready to unravel the complexities of economic geography and spatial inequality within the realm of urban and regional economics. The air is filled with a mix of anticipation and contemplation as the residents gather once more, eager to explore the landscape of opportunity and disparity.

Kato stands before the assembled crowd, his voice echoing with empathy and resolve. "Good morning, my friends. Today, we venture into the terrain of economic geography—mapping the contours of opportunity and disparity that shape the spatial distribution of wealth and well-being. Together, we shall navigate the pathways of progress and strive for a future where prosperity knows no bounds."

He begins with a reflective tone. "In the tapestry of human civilization, economic geography tells the story of how resources, industries, and people are distributed across space. From the clustering of businesses in urban centers to the disparities in access to education and healthcare, these spatial patterns shape the economic landscape and determine the opportunities available to individuals and communities. But let us not overlook the complexities of economic geography, for within them lie both challenges and opportunities that demand our attention and action."

The crowd listens intently, their faces reflecting a mix of curiosity and concern.

"Economic geography," Kato explains, "examines the spatial organization of economic activity and the factors that influence the distribution of resources, industries, and opportunities. From natural endowments and historical legacies to policy interventions and market forces, these factors shape the economic landscapes of cities, regions, and nations, driving both convergence and divergence in economic outcomes."

He gestures to the nearby marketplace, where vendors discuss the impacts of spatial inequality amidst whispers of determination and solidarity. "In Ndola, we witness the effects of spatial inequality on our own community—from the disparities in access to basic services to the uneven distribution of economic opportunities. These challenges not only demand equitable solutions but also underscore the importance of addressing spatial disparities to promote inclusive growth and sustainable development."

Kato then turns his attention to the importance of addressing spatial inequality. "Beyond the patterns," he explains, "lie the implications for social cohesion, economic development, and environmental sustainability. By understanding and addressing spatial inequality, communities can unlock the full potential of their resources, talents, and aspirations, fostering inclusive growth, shared prosperity, and vibrant, resilient communities."

A concerned community leader named Tembo raises her hand. "But how do we address spatial inequality in a way that is equitable and sustainable? Are there any strategies for promoting inclusive economic development and reducing disparities between regions?"

Kato's expression softens with empathy. "Ah, Tembo, a crucial question indeed. Addressing spatial inequality requires a multi-faceted approach that integrates economic, social, and environmental considerations into regional planning and development strategies. By prioritizing investments in infrastructure, education, healthcare, and economic diversification, communities can create opportunities for all residents to thrive, regardless of where they live."

He shares stories of successful initiatives that have embraced inclusive economic development principles, from regional investment funds that support entrepreneurship and innovation to community-driven development projects that empower marginalized communities. "By embracing the challenges of economic geography," Kato says, nodding to the crowd, "we can build regions that are not only prosperous and resilient but also inclusive and sustainable for generations to come."

The audience nods in agreement, their faces reflecting a sense of understanding and determination.

Kato concludes with a call to action. "Let us embrace the

complexities of economic geography as opportunities for positive change. By working together and fostering a culture of collaboration, innovation, and solidarity, we can build regions that are worthy of our aspirations and reflective of our values."

As the session draws to a close, the crowd is filled with a renewed sense of hope and determination. With economic geography as their guide and community as their support, they disperse into the morning, ready to confront the challenges and opportunities of building regions that are truly worthy of their residents' dreams and aspirations.

Kato watches them go, his heart swelling with pride. He knows that with determination as their compass and collaboration as their strength, the residents of Ndola can build regions that are not only prosperous and resilient but also inclusive and sustainable for generations to come.

Housing Markets and Urban Development

"Roofs Over Dreams: Exploring Housing Markets and Urban Development"

As the day unfolds in Ndola, Kato returns to the community center, ready to unravel the dynamics of housing markets and urban development within the realm of urban and regional economics. The atmosphere buzzes with anticipation and contemplation as the residents gather once more, eager to explore the pathways to secure shelter and vibrant communities.

Kato stands before the assembled crowd, his voice resonating with empathy and determination. "Good afternoon, my friends. Today, we embark on a journey into the realm of housing markets and urban development—exploring the forces that shape access to shelter and the evolution of our cities. Together, we shall navigate the pathways to secure homes and vibrant communities for all."

He begins with a reflective tone. "In the fabric of urban life, housing markets play a central role in shaping the spatial, social, and economic dynamics of cities. From the affordability of housing to the quality of neighborhoods, these markets determine not only where we live but also how we live. But let us not overlook the complexities of housing markets, for within them lie both challenges and opportunities that demand our attention and action."

The crowd listens intently, their faces reflecting a mix of curiosity and concern.

"Housing markets," Kato explains, "are shaped by a complex interplay of factors, including supply and demand dynamics, government policies, and socio-economic trends. From the availability of land and construction costs to population growth and income levels, these factors influence housing affordability, accessibility, and quality, driving both opportunities for homeownership and challenges for housing security."

He gestures to the nearby marketplace, where vendors discuss the impacts of housing markets amidst whispers of determination and solidarity. "In Ndola, we witness the effects of housing markets on our own community—from the growth of informal settlements to the pressures on urban infrastructure and services. These challenges not only demand innovative solutions but also underscore the importance of housing as a fundamental human right and a cornerstone of sustainable urban development."

Kato then turns his attention to the importance of addressing housing challenges. "Beyond the markets," he explains, "lie the implications for social inclusion, economic prosperity, and environmental sustainability. By understanding and addressing housing challenges, communities can unlock the full potential of their residents, fostering vibrant, resilient, and inclusive neighborhoods where everyone has the opportunity to thrive."

A concerned community organizer named Mwansa raises her hand. "But how do we address housing challenges in a way that is equitable and sustainable? Are there any strategies for promoting affordable housing and community development?"

Kato's expression softens with empathy. "Ah, Mwansa, a crucial question indeed. Addressing housing challenges requires a multi-faceted approach that integrates social equity, environmental sustainability, and economic resilience into urban planning and development strategies. By prioritizing investments in affordable housing, mixed-income neighborhoods, and community facilities, communities can create inclusive, livable, and vibrant urban spaces for all residents."

He shares stories of successful initiatives that have embraced inclusive housing development principles, from public-private partnerships that provide affordable housing to community land trusts that empower residents to steward their neighborhoods. "By embracing the challenges of housing markets," Kato says, nodding to the crowd, "we can build cities that are not only places of shelter but also beacons of opportunity, diversity, and resilience."

The audience nods in agreement, their faces reflecting a sense of understanding and determination.

Kato concludes with a call to action. "Let us embrace the

complexities of housing markets as opportunities for positive change. By working together and fostering a culture of collaboration, innovation, and solidarity, we can build cities where everyone has a place to call home and the opportunity to build a better future."

As the session draws to a close, the crowd is filled with a renewed sense of hope and determination. With housing markets as their guide and community as their support, they disperse into the afternoon, ready to confront the challenges and opportunities of building cities that are truly worthy of their residents' dreams and aspirations.

Kato watches them go, his heart swelling with pride. He knows that with determination as their compass and collaboration as their strength, the residents of Ndola can build cities that are not only prosperous and resilient but also inclusive and sustainable for generations to come.

Transportation Economics and Infrastructure Investment

"Paths to Progress: Navigating Transportation Economics and Infrastructure Investment"

As the sun dips below the horizon in Ndola, Kato returns to the community center, ready to explore the intricacies of transportation economics and infrastructure investment within the realm of urban and regional economics. The air is filled with a sense of anticipation and determination as the residents gather once more, eager to pave the way for accessible and efficient transportation systems.

Kato stands before the assembled crowd, his voice echoing

with empathy and resolve. "Good evening, my friends. Today, we venture into the realm of transportation economics—exploring the arteries that connect our cities and regions, and the engines that drive our economies forward. Together, we shall chart a course towards accessible, efficient, and sustainable transportation systems for all."

He begins with a reflective tone. "In the tapestry of urban life, transportation systems serve as the lifeblood that sustains the flow of people, goods, and ideas. From roads and railways to ports and airports, these systems enable economic activity, foster social connectivity, and shape the spatial organization of our communities. But let us not overlook the complexities of transportation economics, for within them lie both challenges and opportunities that demand our attention and action."

The crowd listens intently, their faces reflecting a mix of curiosity and concern.

"Transportation economics," Kato explains, "examines the economic principles that govern the supply and demand of transportation services, the efficiency of transportation networks, and the impacts of transportation policies and investments on economic development and social welfare. From the cost-benefit analysis of infrastructure projects to the pricing mechanisms of transit systems, these principles shape the accessibility, affordability, and sustainability of transportation systems."

He gestures to the nearby marketplace, where vendors discuss the impacts of transportation systems amidst whispers of determination and collaboration. "In Ndola, we witness the effects of transportation systems on our own community—from the congestion on our roads to the accessibility of public transit. These challenges not only demand innovative solutions but also underscore the importance of transportation as a driver of economic growth, social inclusion, and environmental sustainability."

Kato then turns his attention to the importance of addressing transportation challenges. "Beyond the principles," he explains, "lie the implications for mobility, accessibility, and environmental stewardship. By understanding and addressing transportation challenges, communities can unlock the full potential of their transportation systems, fostering economic competitiveness, social equity, and environmental resilience."

A concerned community planner named Chanda raises her hand. "But how do we address transportation challenges in a way that is equitable and sustainable? Are there any strategies for promoting accessible and efficient transportation systems for all residents?"

Kato's expression softens with empathy. "Ah, Chanda, a crucial question indeed. Addressing transportation challenges requires a multi-faceted approach that integrates social equity, environmental sustainability, and economic efficiency into transportation planning and investment strategies. By prioritizing investments in public transit, pedestrian infrastructure, and non-motorized transportation options, communities can create accessible, efficient, and sustainable transportation systems that serve the needs of all residents."

He shares stories of successful initiatives that have embraced inclusive transportation planning principles, from bus rapid transit systems that provide affordable and reliable mobility to bike-sharing programs that promote active transportation and reduce carbon emissions. "By embracing the challenges of transportation economics," Kato says, nodding to the crowd, "we can build cities that are not only connected but also compassionate, resilient, and sustainable."

The audience nods in agreement, their faces reflecting a sense of understanding and determination.

Kato concludes with a call to action. "Let us embrace the complexities of transportation economics as opportunities for positive change. By working together and fostering a culture of collaboration, innovation, and solidarity, we can build cities where everyone has access to safe, efficient, and sustainable transportation options, enabling them to reach their full potential and contribute to the collective prosperity of our communities."

As the session draws to a close, the crowd is filled with a renewed sense of hope and determination. With transportation economics as their guide and community as their support, they disperse into the night, ready to confront the challenges and opportunities of building cities that are truly worthy of their residents' dreams and aspirations.

Kato watches them go, his heart swelling with pride. He knows that with determination as their compass and collaboration as their strength, the residents of Ndola can build cities that are not only prosperous and connected but also inclusive and sustainable for generations to come.

Smart Cities and Digital Urban Planning

"Blueprints of Tomorrow: Pioneering Smart Cities and Digital Urban Planning"

Underneath the twinkling stars of Ndola's night sky, Kato returns to the community center, ready to delve into the realm of smart cities and digital urban planning within the context of urban and regional economics. Excitement fills the air as the residents gather once more, eager to embark on a journey towards innovative and sustainable urban futures.

Kato stands before the assembled crowd, his voice carrying the fervor of innovation and progress. "Good evening, my friends. Today, we set forth on a voyage into the world of smart cities and digital urban planning—exploring the frontiers of technology and imagination that will shape the cities of tomorrow. Together, we shall chart a course towards inclusive, resilient, and sustainable urban environments for all."

He begins with a reflective tone. "In the tapestry of urban life, smart cities represent the pinnacle of human ingenuity and technological advancement. From interconnected sensors and data analytics to digital platforms and smart infrastructure, these technologies hold the promise of revolutionizing the way we live, work, and interact in our cities. But let us not overlook the complexities of smart cities and digital urban planning, for within them lie both challenges and opportunities that demand our attention and action."

The crowd listens intently, their faces illuminated by the glow of anticipation.

"Smart cities," Kato explains, "embrace digital technologies to enhance efficiency, improve service delivery, and foster innovation in urban governance and management. From smart transportation systems and energy-efficient buildings to digital platforms for citizen engagement and participatory planning, these innovations have the potential to transform our cities into vibrant, livable, and sustainable spaces for all."

He gestures to the nearby marketplace, where vendors discuss the potential of smart technologies amidst whispers of excitement and curiosity. "In Ndola, we stand at the threshold of a new era of urban development—a future where data-driven insights and digital solutions can address longstanding challenges and unlock new opportunities for economic growth, social inclusion, and environmental sustainability."

Kato then turns his attention to the importance of embracing smart cities and digital urban planning. "Beyond the technologies," he explains, "lie the implications for governance, equity, and resilience. By harnessing the power of digital innovation and data-driven decision-making, communities can create more inclusive, efficient, and sustainable urban environments that serve the needs and aspirations of all residents."

A forward-thinking entrepreneur named Mulenga raises her hand. "But how do we ensure that smart cities are truly inclusive and equitable? Are there any strategies for ensuring that digital technologies benefit all residents, regardless of income or background?"

Kato's expression softens with empathy. "Ah, Mulenga, a crucial question indeed. Ensuring inclusive smart cities requires a commitment to principles such as accessibility, affordability, and social equity. By prioritizing digital literacy, bridging the digital divide, and engaging marginalized communities in the design and implementation of smart city initiatives, communities can ensure that the benefits of digital innovation are shared by all."

He shares stories of successful initiatives that have embraced inclusive smart city principles, from digital literacy programs that empower residents to participate in the digital economy to open data platforms that promote transparency and accountability in urban governance. "By embracing the challenges of smart cities and digital urban planning," Kato says, nodding to the crowd, "we can build cities that are not only technologically advanced but also inclusive, resilient, and sustainable for generations to come."

The audience nods in agreement, their faces reflecting a sense of understanding and determination.

Kato concludes with a call to action. "Let us embrace the possibilities of smart cities and digital urban planning as opportunities for positive change. By working together and fostering a culture of collaboration, innovation, and inclusivity, we can build cities that are not only smart but also compassionate, resilient, and sustainable."

As the session draws to a close, the crowd is filled with a renewed sense of hope and determination. With smart cities as their guide and community as their support, they disperse into the night, ready to confront the challenges and opportunities of building cities that are truly worthy of their residents' dreams and aspirations.

Kato watches them go, his heart swelling with pride. He knows that with determination as their compass and collaboration as their strength, the residents of Ndola can build cities that are not only technologically advanced but also inclusive and sustainable for generations to come.

12

Chapter 12: Health Economics

Healthcare Systems and Market Failures

"Healing Economies: Navigating Healthcare Systems and Market Failures"

The morning sun rises over Ndola, casting a warm glow on the community center where Kato is preparing to discuss a topic close to the hearts of many residents—health economics. The atmosphere is filled with a mix of hope and concern as the community gathers once more, ready to explore the intricacies of healthcare systems and market failures.

Kato stands before the assembled crowd, his voice imbued with empathy and resolve. "Good morning, my friends. Today, we delve into the world of health economics—examining the foundations of healthcare systems and the market failures that challenge their effectiveness. Together, we shall navigate the complexities of ensuring accessible, affordable, and high-quality healthcare for all."

He begins with a reflective tone. "In the fabric of our lives, healthcare systems serve as the pillars that support our well-being and resilience. From hospitals and clinics to insurance schemes and public health initiatives, these systems are designed to provide care and protection against illness and injury. But let us not overlook the market failures that often undermine these goals, for within them lie both challenges and opportunities that demand our attention and action."

The crowd listens intently, their faces reflecting a mix of curiosity and concern.

"Healthcare systems," Kato explains, "are characterized by a unique set of challenges that distinguish them from other sectors of the economy. Market failures such as information asymmetry, moral hazard, and adverse selection often prevent healthcare markets from functioning efficiently, leading to issues like inequitable access, high costs, and varying quality of care."

He gestures to the nearby marketplace, where vendors discuss the impacts of healthcare challenges amidst whispers of determination and solidarity. "In Ndola, we witness the effects of these market failures on our own community—from the high cost of medical care to the lack of access to essential health services. These challenges not only demand innovative solutions but also underscore the importance of healthcare as a fundamental human right and a cornerstone of social justice."

Kato then turns his attention to the importance of addressing healthcare market failures. "Beyond the economic principles," he explains, "lie the implications for health equity, social cohesion, and human dignity. By understanding and addressing the market failures in healthcare, communities can create more inclusive, equitable, and effective healthcare systems that serve the needs and aspirations of all residents."

A concerned nurse named Agnes raises her hand. "But how do we address these market failures in a way that ensures access to quality healthcare for all? Are there any strategies for improving our healthcare system and making it more equitable?"

Kato's expression softens with empathy. "Ah, Agnes, a crucial question indeed. Addressing market failures in healthcare requires a multi-faceted approach that integrates policy interventions, public investments, and community engagement. By strengthening public healthcare systems, regulating private providers, and promoting health literacy, communities can ensure that healthcare services are accessible, affordable, and of high quality."

He shares stories of successful initiatives that have embraced inclusive healthcare principles, from community health programs that provide preventive care to regulatory frameworks that ensure transparency and accountability in healthcare delivery. "By embracing the challenges of healthcare market failures," Kato says, nodding to the crowd, "we can build healthcare systems that are not only efficient but also compassionate, equitable, and resilient."

The audience nods in agreement, their faces reflecting a sense of understanding and determination.

Kato concludes with a call to action. "Let us embrace the complexities of healthcare systems and market failures as opportunities for positive change. By working together and fostering a culture of collaboration, innovation, and solidarity, we can build healthcare systems that are truly worthy of our residents' trust and aspirations."

As the session draws to a close, the crowd is filled with a renewed sense of hope and determination. With healthcare economics as their guide and community as their support, they disperse into the day, ready to confront the challenges and opportunities of building healthcare systems that are truly equitable and effective.

Kato watches them go, his heart swelling with pride. He knows that with determination as their compass and collaboration as their strength, the residents of Ndola can build healthcare systems that are not only sustainable but also inclusive and just for generations to come.

The Economics of Healthcare Financing

"Sustaining Health: The Economics of Healthcare Financing"

As the afternoon sun casts long shadows over Ndola, Kato returns to the community center, ready to address another crucial aspect of health economics: healthcare financing. The air is thick with anticipation as residents gather once more, keen to understand the mechanisms that sustain their healthcare system and explore ways to make it more robust and equitable.

Kato stands before the assembled crowd, his voice filled with determination and clarity. "Good afternoon, my friends. Today, we venture deeper into health economics by examining the economics of healthcare financing—how resources are mobilized, allocated, and utilized to sustain our healthcare systems. Together, we shall uncover the principles and strategies that ensure financial sustainability and equity in healthcare."

He begins with a reflective tone. "In the intricate web of healthcare, financing serves as the lifeline that sustains the system. From public funding and private insurance to out-of-pocket payments and donor contributions, these financial mechanisms determine the accessibility, affordability, and quality of healthcare services. But let us not overlook the complexities and challenges of healthcare financing, for within them lie both obstacles and opportunities that demand our attention and action."

The crowd listens intently, their faces a mix of curiosity and resolve.

"Healthcare financing," Kato explains, "involves the mobilization of resources from various sources to fund health services and ensure financial protection for individuals. The primary models include tax-based systems, social health insurance, private health insurance, and out-of-pocket payments. Each model has its strengths and weaknesses, impacting equity, efficiency, and sustainability in different ways."

He gestures to the nearby marketplace, where vendors discuss the impacts of healthcare financing amidst whispers of concern and hope. "In Ndola, we see the effects of these financing mechanisms firsthand—from the burden of out-of-pocket payments on families to the challenges of ensuring sufficient public funding for health services. These issues not only demand innovative solutions but also underscore the importance of healthcare financing as a foundation for health equity and social justice."

Kato then turns his attention to the importance of effective healthcare financing. "Beyond the models," he explains, "lie the implications for access, affordability, and sustainability. By understanding and improving healthcare financing, communities can create more inclusive and resilient health systems that serve the needs and aspirations of all residents."

A thoughtful economist named Mwansa raises his hand. "But how do we design and implement financing mechanisms that are both equitable and sustainable? Are there any strategies for ensuring that healthcare financing supports universal health coverage?"

Kato's expression brightens with purpose. "Ah, Mwansa, an essential question indeed. Designing and implementing equitable and sustainable healthcare financing requires a multi-faceted approach that integrates principles of fairness, efficiency, and solidarity. By expanding public funding, implementing progressive taxation, promoting social health insurance, and protecting against catastrophic health expenditures, communities can ensure that healthcare financing supports universal health coverage."

He shares stories of successful initiatives that have embraced inclusive financing principles, from national health insurance schemes that pool risks and resources to community-based health financing models that promote solidarity and mutual aid. "By addressing the challenges of healthcare financing," Kato says, nodding to the crowd, "we can build health systems that are not only financially sustainable but also inclusive, equitable, and resilient."

The audience nods in agreement, their faces reflecting a sense of understanding and determination.

Kato concludes with a call to action. "Let us embrace the complexities of healthcare financing as opportunities for positive change. By working together and fostering a culture of collaboration, innovation, and solidarity, we can build healthcare systems that are truly worthy of our residents' trust and aspirations."

As the session draws to a close, the crowd is filled with a renewed sense of hope and determination. With healthcare financing as their guide and community as their support, they disperse into the afternoon, ready to confront the challenges and opportunities of building healthcare systems that are truly equitable and sustainable.

Kato watches them go, his heart swelling with pride. He knows that with determination as their compass and collaboration as their strength, the residents of Ndola can build healthcare systems that are not only financially sustainable but also inclusive and just for generations to come.

Healthcare Costs and Pricing Mechanisms

"Balancing the Scales: Healthcare Costs and Pricing Mechanisms"

As dusk settles over Ndola, Kato returns to the community center for another enlightening session on health economics. The residents, filled with anticipation, gather to explore the intricate and often daunting world of healthcare costs and pricing mechanisms. The room buzzes with the energy of a community eager to understand how to navigate the financial landscape of healthcare.

Kato stands before the attentive crowd, his voice resonating with empathy and insight. "Good evening, my friends. Tonight, we delve into the realm of healthcare costs and pricing mechanisms—examining how costs are determined, controlled, and managed within our healthcare systems. Together, we shall uncover the principles and strategies that ensure healthcare remains affordable and accessible for all."

He begins with a reflective tone. "In the complex ecosystem of healthcare, costs and pricing mechanisms play a pivotal role in determining access to services and the financial burden on individuals and families. From the costs of medical treatments and pharmaceuticals to the pricing strategies of hospitals and insurance companies, these factors shape the landscape of healthcare delivery and affordability. But let us not overlook the complexities of healthcare costs and pricing, for within them lie both challenges and opportunities that demand our attention and action."

The crowd listens intently, their faces a mix of curiosity and concern.

"Healthcare costs," Kato explains, "are influenced by a multitude of factors, including the prices of medical goods and services, the efficiency of healthcare delivery, and the regulatory environment. Pricing mechanisms, on the other hand, involve the methods used to set prices for healthcare services, which can vary significantly across different health systems and markets."

He gestures to the nearby marketplace, where vendors discuss the impacts of healthcare costs amidst whispers of worry and hope. "In Ndola, we witness the burden of healthcare costs on our own community—from the high prices of medications to the financial strain of hospital bills. These challenges not only demand innovative solutions but also underscore the importance of transparent and fair pricing mechanisms in healthcare."

Kato then turns his attention to the importance of understanding and managing healthcare costs and pricing. "Beyond the numbers," he explains, "lie the implications for equity, access, and quality of care. By understanding and addressing healthcare costs and pricing mechanisms, communities can create more affordable and efficient healthcare systems that serve the needs and aspirations of all residents."

A concerned patient named Chanda raises her hand. "But how do we ensure that healthcare costs are kept under control without compromising the quality of care? Are there any strategies for making healthcare more affordable for everyone?"

Kato's expression softens with empathy. "Ah, Chanda, an essential question indeed. Ensuring that healthcare costs are controlled without compromising quality requires a multifaceted approach that integrates cost-containment measures, efficient healthcare delivery, and fair pricing strategies. By promoting value-based care, regulating pharmaceutical prices, and increasing transparency in healthcare pricing, communities can make healthcare more affordable and accessible."

He shares stories of successful initiatives that have embraced cost-containment and fair pricing principles, from value-based pricing models that link payments to health outcomes to policies that promote generic medications and reduce drug prices. "By addressing the challenges of healthcare costs and pricing," Kato says, nodding to the crowd, "we can build health systems that are not only efficient but also compassionate, equitable, and sustainable."

The audience nods in agreement, their faces reflecting a sense of understanding and determination.

Kato concludes with a call to action. "Let us embrace the complexities of healthcare costs and pricing mechanisms as opportunities for positive change. By working together and fostering a culture of collaboration, innovation, and transparency, we can build healthcare systems that are truly worthy of our residents' trust and aspirations."

As the session draws to a close, the crowd is filled with a renewed sense of hope and determination. With healthcare costs and pricing as their guide and community as their support, they disperse into the night, ready to confront the challenges and opportunities of building healthcare systems that are truly affordable and accessible.

Kato watches them go, his heart swelling with pride. He knows that with determination as their compass and collaboration as their strength, the residents of Ndola can build healthcare systems that are not only financially sustainable but also inclusive and just for generations to come.

Health Insurance Markets and Risk Pooling

"Shared Risks, Shared Rewards: Health Insurance Markets and Risk Pooling"

Under the soft glow of the streetlights, Ndola's community center is once again abuzz with anticipation. Residents gather for another pivotal discussion, this time focusing on the complexities of health insurance markets and the concept of risk pooling. The room is filled with a mix of hope, curiosity, and a collective desire to understand how these mechanisms can be leveraged to ensure better health outcomes for everyone.

Kato stands at the front, his demeanor both calm and resolute. "Good evening, everyone. Tonight, we explore the world of health insurance markets and the crucial role of risk pooling. Our goal is to understand how these systems work to spread financial risk across communities, making healthcare more affordable and accessible for all."

He begins with a reflective tone. "Health insurance is a fundamental component of modern healthcare systems. It serves as a financial safety net, protecting individuals from the high costs of medical care. However, the effectiveness of health insurance largely depends on the principles of risk pooling, where risks and costs are shared among a large group of people."

The crowd listens intently, their faces a mix of curiosity and determination.

"Risk pooling," Kato explains, "is the process by which insurance spreads the financial risk of health expenses across all the insured individuals. By pooling risks, health insurance can provide coverage for everyone, including those who may require more medical care. This collective approach helps to ensure that healthcare costs are manageable for each individual."

He gestures to the nearby marketplace, where vendors discuss the impacts of health insurance amidst whispers of solidarity and hope. "In Ndola, many families face the challenge of high healthcare costs without adequate insurance coverage. Understanding and improving health insurance markets and risk pooling can help us create a system where everyone has access to affordable healthcare."

Kato then turns his attention to the importance of effective health insurance and risk pooling. "Beyond the mechanics of insurance," he explains, "lie the implications for equity, access, and financial protection. By understanding and optimizing health insurance markets and risk pooling, communities can create more resilient healthcare systems that serve the needs and aspirations of all residents."

A thoughtful young doctor named Alex raises his hand. "But how do we ensure that health insurance markets are fair and that risk pooling effectively protects the most vulnerable? Are there any strategies for improving our health insurance system?"

Kato's expression brightens with purpose. "Ah, Alex, an excellent question. Ensuring that health insurance markets are fair and that risk pooling is effective requires a multi-faceted approach. This includes regulatory frameworks to prevent discrimination based on health status, subsidies to make insurance affordable for low-income individuals, and public awareness campaigns to encourage widespread participation in insurance programs."

He shares stories of successful initiatives that have embraced inclusive insurance principles, from community-based health insurance schemes that pool risks locally to national health insurance programs that provide universal coverage. "By addressing the challenges of health insurance markets and risk pooling," Kato says, nodding to the crowd, "we can build health systems that are not only inclusive but also financially sustainable and resilient."

The audience nods in agreement, their faces reflecting a sense of understanding and determination.

Kato concludes with a call to action. "Let us embrace the complexities of health insurance markets and risk pooling as opportunities for positive change. By working together and fostering a culture of collaboration, innovation, and solidarity, we can build healthcare systems that are truly worthy of our residents' trust and aspirations."

As the session draws to a close, the crowd is filled with a renewed sense of hope and determination. With health insurance markets and risk pooling as their guide and community as their support, they disperse into the evening, ready to confront the challenges and opportunities of building healthcare systems that are truly equitable and accessible.

Kato watches them go, his heart swelling with pride. He knows that with determination as their compass and collaboration as their strength, the residents of Ndola can build healthcare systems that are not only financially sustainable but also inclusive and just for generations to come.

Public Health Policy and Disease Prevention

"Prevention for Prosperity: Public Health Policy and Disease Prevention"

As the golden hues of the sunset give way to twilight, Ndola's community center once again becomes the heart of lively discussion and eager learning. The topic of the evening is crucial: public health policy and disease prevention. The residents, filled with a sense of urgency and hope, gather to explore how proactive measures can safeguard their health and enhance their community's well-being.

Kato stands at the front, his voice imbued with both passion and pragmatism. "Good evening, everyone. Tonight, we embark on a journey into the realm of public health policy and disease prevention. Our goal is to understand how policies and preventative measures can protect our health, reduce disease burden, and foster a healthier, more resilient community."

He begins with a reflective tone. "Public health policy and disease prevention are cornerstones of a robust healthcare system. By focusing on prevention rather than cure, we can significantly reduce healthcare costs, improve quality of life, and ensure long-term health sustainability. But let us not overlook the complexities and challenges of crafting effective public health policies, for within them lie both obstacles and opportunities that demand our attention and action."

The crowd listens intently, their faces a mix of curiosity and resolve.

"Public health policy," Kato explains, "involves the development and implementation of strategies to promote health, prevent disease, and prolong life. Effective policies are based on sound scientific evidence and aim to address health determinants, such as environment, lifestyle, and socioeconomic factors."

He gestures to the nearby marketplace, where vendors discuss the impacts of public health amidst whispers of concern and hope. "In Ndola, we face various health challenges—from infectious diseases and malnutrition to non-communicable diseases and environmental hazards. Crafting and implementing effective public health policies can help us address these challenges proactively, reducing disease burden and enhancing our community's well-being."

Kato then turns his attention to the importance of disease prevention. "Prevention," he explains, "is always better than cure. By focusing on preventive measures, such as vaccination programs, health education, and sanitation improvements, we can significantly reduce the incidence of disease and improve overall health outcomes."

A concerned mother named Maria raises her hand. "But how do we ensure that public health policies are effective and that disease prevention measures reach everyone, especially the most vulnerable? Are there any strategies for enhancing public health in our community?"

Kato's expression softens with empathy. "Ah, Maria, an essential question indeed. Ensuring that public health policies are effective and that disease prevention measures are inclusive requires a multi-faceted approach. This includes strengthening healthcare infrastructure, increasing public health funding, and fostering community engagement. Additionally, health education campaigns and collaboration with local leaders can ensure that prevention measures are understood and adopted by all."

He shares stories of successful public health initiatives, from vaccination drives that have eradicated diseases to community-based programs that promote healthy lifestyles and environmental cleanliness. "By addressing the challenges of public health policy and disease prevention," Kato says, nodding to the crowd, "we can build health systems that are not only proactive but also equitable and resilient."

The audience nods in agreement, their faces reflecting a sense of understanding and determination.

Kato concludes with a call to action. "Let us embrace the complexities of public health policy and disease prevention as opportunities for positive change. By working together and fostering a culture of collaboration, innovation, and solidarity, we can build healthcare systems that are truly worthy of our residents' trust and aspirations."

As the session draws to a close, the crowd is filled with a renewed sense of hope and determination. With public health policy and disease prevention as their guide and community as their support, they disperse into the night, ready to confront the challenges and opportunities of building healthcare systems that are truly proactive and inclusive.

Kato watches them go, his heart swelling with pride. He knows that with determination as their compass and collaboration as their strength, the residents of Ndola can build healthcare systems that are not only financially sustainable but also inclusive and just for generations to come.

Global Health Economics and Pandemic Preparedness

"Guardians of the Globe: Global Health Economics and Pandemic Preparedness"

As the stars begin to twinkle in the clear night sky over Ndola, the community center lights up with the anticipation of a vital discussion. Tonight's session on global health economics and pandemic preparedness brings together residents eager to understand how global dynamics affect local health and how their community can be better prepared for future health crises.

Kato stands before the gathered community, his voice steady and filled with conviction. "Good evening, everyone. Tonight, we delve into the crucial topic of global health economics and pandemic preparedness. Our aim is to understand how global health policies impact us here in Ndola and what we can do to prepare for and mitigate the effects of future pandemics."

He begins with a reflective tone. "The interconnected nature of our world means that health issues in one part of the globe can quickly become global concerns. Pandemics like COVID-

19 have shown us the importance of global health cooperation, economic resilience, and robust preparedness plans. But let us not overlook the complexities and challenges of global health economics, for within them lie both obstacles and opportunities that demand our attention and action."

The crowd listens intently, their faces a mix of curiosity and concern.

"Global health economics," Kato explains, "involves the study of how health and healthcare are influenced by global economic factors. It includes the allocation of resources for health services, the economic impact of health policies, and the financial aspects of disease prevention and control on a global scale."

He gestures to the nearby marketplace, where vendors discuss the impacts of global health amidst whispers of worry and hope. "In Ndola, we have felt the ripple effects of global health crises—from supply chain disruptions to increased healthcare costs. Understanding global health economics can help us better navigate these challenges and advocate for more effective global health policies."

Kato then turns his attention to pandemic preparedness. "Pandemic preparedness," he explains, "involves planning and implementing strategies to prevent, detect, and respond to infectious disease outbreaks. Effective preparedness can save lives, protect economies, and ensure that healthcare systems remain resilient during crises."

A concerned nurse named Naomi raises her hand. "But how do we ensure that our community is prepared for future pandemics, especially given our limited resources? Are there any strategies for enhancing our preparedness?"

Kato's expression brightens with purpose. "Ah, Naomi, an

excellent question. Ensuring that our community is prepared for future pandemics requires a multi-faceted approach. This includes strengthening our healthcare infrastructure, improving disease surveillance, and fostering international cooperation. Additionally, public education campaigns and community engagement are crucial for ensuring that preparedness measures are understood and adopted by all."

He shares stories of successful pandemic preparedness initiatives, from international collaborations that have developed early warning systems to local programs that train healthcare workers and educate the public about hygiene and vaccination. "By addressing the challenges of global health economics and pandemic preparedness," Kato says, nodding to the crowd, "we can build health systems that are not only proactive but also resilient and adaptable."

The audience nods in agreement, their faces reflecting a sense of understanding and determination.

Kato concludes with a call to action. "Let us embrace the complexities of global health economics and pandemic preparedness as opportunities for positive change. By working together and fostering a culture of collaboration, innovation, and solidarity, we can build healthcare systems that are truly capable of withstanding future health crises."

As the session draws to a close, the crowd is filled with a renewed sense of hope and determination. With global health economics and pandemic preparedness as their guide and community as their support, they disperse into the night, ready to confront the challenges and opportunities of building healthcare systems that are truly resilient and inclusive.

Kato watches them go, his heart swelling with pride. He knows that with determination as their compass and collaboration as their strength, the residents of Ndola can build healthcare systems that are not only financially sustainable but also inclusive and just for generations to come.

13

Chapter 13: Economic Policy Analysis

The Policy Process and Economic Decision-Making

"Crafting Change: The Policy Process and Economic Decision-Making"

As the early morning sun casts a golden hue over Ndola, the community center is already bustling with activity. Today's session on economic policy analysis, focusing on the policy process and economic decision-making, promises to be particularly engaging. Residents are eager to understand how economic policies are crafted and how they can influence these processes to better their community.

Kato stands at the front, his voice brimming with energy and determination. "Good morning, everyone. Today, we explore the intricate world of economic policy analysis, specifically the policy process and economic decision-making. Our goal is to understand how policies are created, the factors that influence these decisions, and how we, as a community, can play an active role in shaping them."

He begins with a reflective tone. "Economic policies shape every aspect of our lives, from the prices we pay for goods to the quality of our healthcare and education. The process of crafting these policies is complex, involving various stages and numerous stakeholders. But let us not be daunted by these complexities, for within them lie both challenges and opportunities for meaningful change."

The crowd listens intently, their faces a mix of curiosity and resolve.

"The policy process," Kato explains, "typically involves several stages: problem identification, policy formulation, policy adoption, implementation, and evaluation. Each stage requires careful analysis, negotiation, and decision-making to ensure that the policies are effective and equitable."

He gestures to the nearby marketplace, where vendors discuss the impacts of economic policies amidst whispers of concern and hope. "In Ndola, economic policies directly affect our livelihoods—from trade regulations that impact our businesses to social policies that determine our access to services. Understanding the policy process allows us to advocate for policies that address our needs and aspirations."

Kato then turns his attention to economic decision-making. "Economic decision-making," he explains, "involves selecting the best course of action from various alternatives to achieve desired economic outcomes. This requires considering both the short-term and long-term impacts of decisions, as well as balancing competing interests and priorities."

A thoughtful young entrepreneur named Musa raises his hand. "But how do we ensure that economic policies reflect the needs of our community and not just the interests of a few? Are there any strategies for influencing policy decisions effectively?"

Kato's expression brightens with purpose. "Ah, Musa, an excellent question. Ensuring that economic policies reflect the needs of our community requires a multi-faceted approach. This includes active participation in public consultations, building coalitions to advocate for common interests, and engaging with policymakers to provide input and feedback. Additionally, using data and evidence to support our positions can help make a compelling case for our needs."

He shares stories of successful community-led initiatives that have influenced economic policy decisions, from grassroots campaigns that have secured funding for local projects to collaborative efforts that have shaped regional development plans. "By understanding the policy process and economic decision-making," Kato says, nodding to the crowd, "we can become effective advocates for our community and ensure that policies are equitable and beneficial for all."

The audience nods in agreement, their faces reflecting a sense of understanding and determination.

Kato concludes with a call to action. "Let us embrace the complexities of the policy process and economic decision-making as opportunities for positive change. By working together and fostering a culture of collaboration, innovation, and solidarity, we can shape economic policies that are truly reflective of our community's needs and aspirations."

As the session draws to a close, the crowd is filled with a renewed sense of hope and determination. With knowledge of the policy process and economic decision-making as their guide and community as their support, they disperse into the morning, ready to confront the challenges and opportunities of shaping policies that are equitable and inclusive.

Kato watches them go, his heart swelling with pride. He knows that with determination as their compass and collaboration as their strength, the residents of Ndola can influence economic policies that are not only beneficial for their community but also just and sustainable for generations to come.

Cost-Benefit Analysis and Policy Evaluation

"Balancing the Scales: Cost-Benefit Analysis and Policy Evaluation"

As the afternoon sun casts long shadows over Ndola, the community center fills once again with eager residents. Today's session on economic policy analysis continues with a focus on cost-benefit analysis and policy evaluation, critical tools for making informed and effective policy decisions.

Kato stands at the front, his voice steady and confident. "Good afternoon, everyone. Today, we delve deeper into economic policy analysis by exploring cost-benefit analysis and policy evaluation. Our goal is to understand how these tools can help us assess the value and impact of policies, ensuring they are both effective and equitable."

He begins with a reflective tone. "Cost-benefit analysis (CBA) is a fundamental tool in economic decision-making. It involves comparing the costs and benefits of a policy to determine whether it is worthwhile. This analysis helps policymakers allocate resources efficiently and make decisions that maximize overall welfare."

The crowd listens attentively, their faces a mix of curiosity and determination.

"CBA," Kato explains, "requires identifying and quantifying all the costs and benefits associated with a policy. This includes direct costs, such as implementation expenses, and indirect costs, like potential negative side effects. Benefits must also be measured, including both tangible outcomes like improved health and intangible ones like enhanced quality of life."

He gestures to the nearby marketplace, where vendors discuss the impacts of economic policies amidst whispers of concern and hope. "In Ndola, applying cost-benefit analysis to our local projects—such as infrastructure improvements or health initiatives—can help us ensure that our resources are used effectively and that the benefits outweigh the costs."

Kato then turns his attention to policy evaluation. "Policy evaluation," he explains, "involves assessing the effectiveness and outcomes of a policy after its implementation. This process helps determine whether the policy has achieved its goals and provides insights for future improvements."

A concerned teacher named Chanda raises her hand. "But how do we ensure that our cost-benefit analyses and policy evaluations are accurate and unbiased? Are there any strategies for conducting these assessments effectively?"

Kato's expression brightens with purpose. "Ah, Chanda, an excellent question. Ensuring accuracy and objectivity in cost-benefit analyses and policy evaluations requires a systematic and transparent approach. This includes collecting reliable data, using robust methodologies, and involving diverse stakeholders in the evaluation process. Additionally, it's crucial to consider both short-term and long-term impacts, as well as distributional effects on different segments of the population."

He shares stories of successful cost-benefit analyses and policy evaluations that have informed better decision-making, from public health interventions that have saved lives and reduced healthcare costs to educational programs that have improved learning outcomes and economic opportunities. "By understanding and applying cost-benefit analysis and policy evaluation," Kato says, nodding to the crowd, "we can make informed decisions that maximize benefits, minimize costs, and promote equity."

The audience nods in agreement, their faces reflecting a sense of understanding and determination.

Kato concludes with a call to action. "Let us embrace the tools of cost-benefit analysis and policy evaluation as opportunities for positive change. By working together and fostering a culture of transparency, accountability, and continuous improvement, we can ensure that our policies are both effective and equitable."

As the session draws to a close, the crowd is filled with a renewed sense of hope and determination. With knowledge of cost-benefit analysis and policy evaluation as their guide and community as their support, they disperse into the afternoon, ready to confront the challenges and opportunities of making informed and effective policy decisions.

Kato watches them go, his heart swelling with pride. He knows that with determination as their compass and collaboration as their strength, the residents of Ndola can make informed decisions that are not only beneficial for their community but also just and sustainable for generations to come.

Regulatory Impact Assessment

"Navigating the Rules: Regulatory Impact Assessment"

As the late afternoon sun bathes Ndola in a warm glow, the community center once again becomes a hub of activity. Residents gather with a palpable sense of anticipation for today's session on economic policy analysis, which will focus on regulatory impact assessment (RIA). This tool is crucial for understanding how regulations affect economic and social outcomes.

Kato stands at the front, his voice calm yet filled with determination. "Good evening, everyone. Today, we explore the concept of regulatory impact assessment, or RIA. Our goal is to understand how this tool can help us evaluate the potential effects of regulations and ensure that they promote positive outcomes for our community."

He begins with a reflective tone. "Regulations are essential for maintaining order, protecting public health, and ensuring fair markets. However, they can also impose costs and unintended consequences. RIA is a systematic process used to evaluate the benefits and costs of proposed regulations before they are implemented. It helps policymakers make informed decisions that balance various interests and impacts."

The crowd listens intently, their faces a mix of curiosity and concern.

"RIA," Kato explains, "involves several steps: identifying the problem that the regulation aims to address, analyzing the potential impacts of different regulatory options, consulting stakeholders, and making recommendations based on the evidence. This process helps ensure that regulations achieve their intended goals without imposing unnecessary burdens."

He gestures to the nearby industrial area, where workers and business owners discuss the impacts of regulations amidst whispers of both frustration and hope. "In Ndola, RIA can help us evaluate the effects of regulations on businesses, workers, and the environment. For example, before implementing new environmental regulations, RIA can help us understand their economic impact on local industries and their effectiveness in improving public health."

Kato then turns his attention to stakeholder engagement. "Engaging stakeholders," he explains, "is a crucial part of RIA. This includes consulting businesses, workers, and community members who will be affected by the regulation. Their input provides valuable insights and helps identify potential issues that may not be evident from a purely technical analysis."

A concerned shop owner named Peter raises his hand. "But how do we ensure that all voices are heard in the regulatory impact assessment process, especially those of small businesses and marginalized groups? Are there any strategies for inclusive stakeholder engagement?"

Kato's expression brightens with purpose. "Ah, Peter, an excellent question. Ensuring inclusive stakeholder engagement in RIA requires proactive outreach and transparent communication. This includes organizing public consultations, conducting surveys, and holding focus group discussions. It's also important to provide clear information about the proposed regulation and its potential impacts, so stakeholders can provide informed feedback."

He shares stories of successful RIAs that have led to better regulations, from environmental policies that have balanced economic growth with sustainability to labor laws that have protected workers' rights while supporting business competitiveness. "By understanding and applying regulatory impact assessment," Kato says, nodding to the crowd, "we can develop regulations that are effective, equitable, and reflective of our community's needs."

The audience nods in agreement, their faces reflecting a sense of understanding and determination.

Kato concludes with a call to action. "Let us embrace the tool of regulatory impact assessment as an opportunity for positive change. By working together and fostering a culture of transparency, accountability, and inclusivity, we can ensure that our regulations promote well-being and fairness for all."

As the session draws to a close, the crowd is filled with a renewed sense of hope and determination. With knowledge of regulatory impact assessment as their guide and community as their support, they disperse into the evening, ready to confront the challenges and opportunities of shaping regulations that are effective and inclusive.

Kato watches them go, his heart swelling with pride. He knows that with determination as their compass and collaboration as their strength, the residents of Ndola can shape regulations that are not only beneficial for their community but also just and sustainable for generations to come.

Political Economy of Policy Reforms

"Navigating Power: The Political Economy of Policy Reforms"

As twilight begins to settle over Ndola, the community center remains vibrant with activity. The residents have returned for the evening session on economic policy analysis, focusing this time on the political economy of policy reforms. The air is filled with anticipation as they prepare to understand the complexities of how power dynamics influence policy changes.

Kato stands before the attentive crowd, his voice resolute and engaging. "Good evening, everyone. Tonight, we will explore the political economy of policy reforms. Our aim is to understand how power, politics, and economic interests intersect in the process of implementing policy changes, and how we can navigate these dynamics to advocate for meaningful reforms."

He begins with a reflective tone. "Policy reforms often require more than just sound economic reasoning. They involve navigating the interests of various stakeholders, addressing political constraints, and managing the distributional impacts of changes. The political economy of policy reforms is about understanding these complexities and finding ways to achieve sustainable and equitable outcomes."

The crowd listens intently, their faces a mix of curiosity and resolve.

"Reforms," Kato explains, "can be contentious because they often challenge existing power structures and vested interests. Successful reforms require building broad coalitions, engaging in strategic negotiation, and sometimes making compromises. It's about finding a balance between what is

CHAPTER 13: ECONOMIC POLICY ANALYSIS

ideal and what is politically feasible."

He gestures to the city hall, where local politicians and community leaders debate policies that could shape the future of Ndola. "In Ndola, understanding the political economy of policy reforms is crucial for addressing issues such as land use, public service delivery, and economic development. By navigating these dynamics effectively, we can advocate for policies that truly benefit our community."

Kato then turns his attention to the role of coalitions. "Building coalitions," he explains, "is essential for advancing policy reforms. This involves bringing together diverse groups with a shared interest in the reform, whether they are community members, businesses, or advocacy organizations. By working together, we can amplify our voice and increase our influence."

A thoughtful activist named Mwansa raises her hand. "But how do we deal with resistance from powerful interests who may oppose the reforms? Are there strategies for overcoming such obstacles?"

Kato's expression brightens with purpose. "Ah, Mwansa, an excellent question. Overcoming resistance requires strategic engagement and negotiation. This includes identifying potential allies within the power structure, framing the reform in a way that highlights its benefits to various stakeholders, and being prepared to make tactical compromises. It's also important to use data and evidence to build a compelling case for the reform."

He shares stories of successful policy reforms that have navigated complex political economies, from land reforms that have empowered local farmers to healthcare initiatives that have improved access to services. "By understanding and engaging with the political economy of policy reforms," Kato says, nodding to the crowd, "we can advocate for changes that are both effective and equitable."

The audience nods in agreement, their faces reflecting a sense of understanding and determination.

Kato concludes with a call to action. "Let us embrace the complexities of the political economy of policy reforms as opportunities for positive change. By building coalitions, engaging strategically, and fostering a culture of collaboration and resilience, we can achieve reforms that are truly beneficial for our community."

As the session draws to a close, the crowd is filled with a renewed sense of hope and determination. With knowledge of the political economy of policy reforms as their guide and community as their support, they disperse into the evening, ready to confront the challenges and opportunities of advocating for meaningful policy changes.

Kato watches them go, his heart swelling with pride. He knows that with determination as their compass and collaboration as their strength, the residents of Ndola can navigate the complexities of power and politics to achieve reforms that are not only beneficial for their community but also just and sustainable for generations to come.

Behavioral Insights in Policy Design

"Shaping Behavior: Harnessing Behavioral Insights in Policy Design"

As night falls over Ndola, the community center remains alight with activity. Residents have gathered once again, eager to delve into the complexities of policy design. Tonight's focus is on the role of behavioral insights—a topic that promises to shed light on how human behavior influences the effectiveness of policies.

Kato stands before the crowd, his voice carrying a sense of intrigue and anticipation. "Good evening, everyone. Tonight, we embark on a fascinating journey into the realm of policy design, exploring the role of behavioral insights. Our goal is to understand how human behavior shapes the outcomes of policies and how we can use this understanding to design more effective interventions."

He begins with a reflective tone. "Human behavior is often influenced by factors beyond rational decision-making, such as cognitive biases, social norms, and emotions. Behavioral insights help us understand these dynamics and design policies that account for them, ultimately leading to better outcomes for society."

The crowd leans in, captivated by Kato's words.

"Behavioral insights," Kato explains, "offer a fresh perspective on policy design by focusing on how people actually behave, rather than how they should behave according to traditional economic models. By incorporating insights from psychology, sociology, and neuroscience, policymakers can design interventions that are more likely to be accepted and effective."

He gestures to the bustling streets of Ndola, where people

go about their daily lives, influenced by countless subtle factors. "In Ndola, understanding behavioral insights is crucial for addressing various social and economic challenges, from promoting healthy behaviors to increasing savings and reducing crime. By harnessing these insights, we can design policies that nudge people towards making better choices for themselves and society."

Kato then turns his attention to the power of choice architecture. "Choice architecture," he explains, "refers to the way in which choices are presented to people and how this influences their decisions. By carefully designing the environment in which choices are made, policymakers can steer people towards more beneficial outcomes without restricting their freedom."

A curious young student named Chipo raises her hand. "But how do we ensure that policies designed with behavioral insights are ethical and respect people's autonomy? Are there risks of manipulation?"

Kato's expression brightens with understanding. "Ah, Chipo, an important question. Ensuring ethical policy design requires transparency, accountability, and a commitment to respecting individual autonomy. Policymakers must be mindful of the potential for unintended consequences and carefully consider the ethical implications of their interventions. It's also important to involve stakeholders in the design process and provide opportunities for feedback and evaluation."

He shares stories of successful policy interventions that have leveraged behavioral insights, from simple changes in default options that have increased organ donation rates to personalized messaging that has encouraged energy conservation.

"By understanding and applying behavioral insights," Kato says, nodding to the crowd, "we can design policies that nudge people towards making choices that are not only better for themselves but also for society as a whole."

The audience nods in agreement, their faces reflecting a sense of understanding and empowerment.

Kato concludes with a call to action. "Let us embrace the power of behavioral insights as a tool for positive change. By designing policies that take into account how people actually behave, we can create a world where making the right choice is not only easier but also more rewarding."

As the session draws to a close, the crowd disperses into the night, their minds buzzing with newfound knowledge and inspiration. With behavioral insights as their guide and community as their support, they are ready to confront the challenges and opportunities of designing policies that truly shape behavior for the better.

Case Studies in Effective Policy Implementation

"Lessons Learned: Case Studies in Effective Policy Implementation"

As the stars twinkle overhead, casting a soft glow over Ndola, the community center remains a beacon of learning and inspiration. Tonight's session on economic policy analysis continues, with a focus on real-world case studies in effective policy implementation. Residents gather once more, eager to glean insights from the experiences of organizations and companies that have successfully navigated the complexities of policy implementation.

Kato stands before the assembled crowd, his voice steady and resolute. "Good evening, everyone. Tonight, we embark on a journey through the annals of policy implementation, exploring real-world case studies of organizations and companies that have achieved remarkable success in translating policy into action. Our goal is to extract valuable lessons that we can apply to our own efforts here in Ndola."

He begins with a reflective tone. "Effective policy implementation requires more than just good intentions. It demands careful planning, strong leadership, and a commitment to adaptability in the face of challenges. By studying the experiences of others, we can gain invaluable insights into what works—and what doesn't—when it comes to turning policy into practice."

The crowd listens intently, their faces illuminated by the flickering light of the candles that adorn the room.

"Our first case study," Kato announces, "takes us to Rwanda, where the government's ambitious healthcare reforms have transformed the country's healthcare system. Through strategic investments in infrastructure, technology, and human resources, as well as innovative financing mechanisms such as community health insurance, Rwanda has achieved remarkable gains in healthcare access and outcomes."

He shares stories of Rwandan organizations such as Partners In Health and the Ministry of Health, whose collaborative efforts have been instrumental in driving these reforms forward. "By prioritizing community engagement, leveraging technology, and fostering partnerships with local and international stakeholders, Rwanda has demonstrated the power of effective policy implementation in improving the lives of its citizens."

Kato then shifts focus to a different continent, highlighting the efforts of a multinational corporation closer to home. "Our second case study takes us to Zambia, where a mining company, Mopani Copper Mines, has implemented a comprehensive community development program aimed at enhancing the well-being of local communities."

He recounts how Mopani Copper Mines has invested in education, healthcare, infrastructure, and small business development, working closely with community leaders and government agencies to ensure that their initiatives align with local priorities and needs. "Through its commitment to corporate social responsibility and sustainable development, Mopani Copper Mines has demonstrated how private sector organizations can play a pivotal role in driving positive social change."

A young entrepreneur named Mulenga raises her hand. "But how do we ensure that policies implemented by large organizations truly benefit local communities and are not just driven by corporate interests? Are there strategies for fostering genuine collaboration and accountability?"

Kato's expression brightens with understanding. "Ah, Mulenga, an excellent question. Ensuring that policies implemented by large organizations benefit local communities requires transparency, accountability, and meaningful engagement with stakeholders. This includes involving community members in decision-making processes, conducting regular impact assessments, and establishing mechanisms for feedback and grievance redressal."

He shares additional case studies from around the world, including examples of successful policy implementation in sectors such as education, environmental conservation, and poverty alleviation. "By studying these diverse experiences," Kato says, nodding to the crowd, "we can glean valuable insights into the principles and practices that underpin effective policy implementation, empowering us to drive positive change right here in Ndola."

The audience nods in agreement, their faces reflecting a sense of inspiration and determination.

Kato concludes with a call to action. "Let us embrace the lessons learned from these case studies as we continue our journey towards meaningful policy implementation. By drawing upon the experiences of others and adapting their strategies to our local context, we can create a future where policies translate into tangible improvements in the lives of our community members."

As the session draws to a close, the crowd disperses into the night, their hearts and minds filled with newfound knowledge and resolve. With real-world case studies as their guide and community as their support, they are ready to embark on the next chapter of their journey towards positive change in Ndola and beyond.

14

Chapter 14: Emerging Trends in Economics

The Rise of Digital Economies

"Navigating the Digital Frontier: The Rise of Digital Economies"

As dawn breaks over Ndola, signaling the start of a new day, the community center buzzes with anticipation. Today's session on emerging trends in economics promises to shed light on the transformative power of digital economies. Residents gather eagerly, eager to explore the opportunities and challenges presented by the digital frontier.

Kato stands before the crowd, his voice filled with excitement and energy. "Good morning, everyone. Today, we embark on a thrilling exploration of emerging trends in economics, beginning with the rise of digital economies. Our goal is to understand how the digital revolution is reshaping the way we live, work, and interact, and how we can navigate this new frontier to build a better future for all."

He begins with a reflective tone. "Digital economies are characterized by the widespread use of digital technologies, such as the internet, smartphones, and artificial intelligence, to conduct economic activities. These technologies have revolutionized the way we produce, consume, and exchange goods and services, opening up new possibilities and opportunities for innovation and growth."

The crowd listens intently, their faces reflecting a mix of curiosity and excitement.

"Digital economies," Kato explains, "have the potential to drive economic development and improve living standards by increasing productivity, expanding access to markets, and fostering entrepreneurship. In Ndola, we are already seeing the impact of digital technologies on sectors such as e-commerce, fintech, and telemedicine, creating new jobs and business opportunities."

He gestures to the bustling marketplace, where vendors use mobile payment apps to conduct transactions and customers browse online stores from the comfort of their homes. "In Ndola, the rise of digital economies is creating new pathways to prosperity, enabling entrepreneurs to reach customers beyond traditional boundaries and empowering individuals to access services that were once out of reach."

Kato then turns his attention to the challenges posed by the digital revolution. "While digital economies offer tremendous opportunities, they also present unique challenges, such as digital divide, data privacy, and cybersecurity. It is essential that we address these challenges proactively to ensure that the benefits of the digital revolution are shared equitably and that no one is left behind."

A concerned community leader named Chanda raises her hand. "But how do we bridge the digital divide and ensure that everyone has access to the opportunities presented by digital economies? Are there strategies for fostering digital inclusion?"

Kato's expression brightens with determination. "Ah, Chanda, an important question. Bridging the digital divide requires a multi-faceted approach that addresses infrastructure, affordability, and digital literacy. This includes investing in broadband infrastructure to expand internet access, reducing the cost of digital devices and services, and providing training and support to help people navigate the digital world."

He shares stories of successful initiatives from around the world that have promoted digital inclusion, from community-led internet access projects to government-sponsored digital skills training programs. "By understanding and addressing the barriers to digital inclusion," Kato says, nodding to the crowd, "we can ensure that everyone has the opportunity to participate in and benefit from the digital economy."

The audience nods in agreement, their faces reflecting a sense of determination and possibility.

Kato concludes with a call to action. "Let us embrace the opportunities presented by digital economies as we continue our journey towards economic prosperity and social inclusion. By harnessing the power of digital technologies to drive innovation and create opportunities for all, we can build a future that is brighter and more inclusive for everyone in Ndola."

As the session draws to a close, the crowd disperses into the morning light, their minds buzzing with excitement and possibility. With the rise of digital economies as their guide and community as their support, they are ready to embrace the opportunities of the digital frontier and shape a future that is both prosperous and equitable.

Platform Economics and Network Effects

"The Power of Connections: Platform Economics and Network Effects"

As the sun climbs higher in the sky, casting a warm glow over Ndola, the community center hums with anticipation. Today's discussion on emerging trends in economics delves into the fascinating world of platform economics and network effects. Residents gather eagerly, ready to explore the transformative impact of connectivity and collaboration in the digital age.

Kato stands at the forefront of the room, his voice filled with enthusiasm and curiosity. "Good afternoon, everyone. Today, we embark on a journey into the realm of platform economics and network effects—a world where connections are currency, and collaboration is king. Our goal is to understand how digital platforms are revolutionizing the way we do business and interact, and how we can harness the power of networks to drive economic growth and innovation."

He begins with a reflective tone. "Platform economics is built on the idea of creating digital ecosystems where producers and consumers can interact and transact with each other. These platforms—whether they be social media networks, online marketplaces, or collaborative workspaces—facilitate connections, enable transactions, and generate value through network effects."

CHAPTER 14: EMERGING TRENDS IN ECONOMICS

The crowd listens intently, their eyes alight with curiosity and anticipation.

"Network effects," Kato explains, "occur when the value of a platform increases as more users join and participate in the network. This creates a virtuous cycle where the platform becomes more valuable to users, attracting even more participants and further enhancing its utility and appeal. In Ndola, we are witnessing the power of network effects in action, as digital platforms such as ride-sharing apps and online marketplaces become integral parts of our daily lives."

He gestures to the group of entrepreneurs gathered in the corner, their heads bent together in animated discussion as they discuss their latest collaboration on a digital platform. "In Ndola, platform economics is driving entrepreneurship and innovation, creating new opportunities for businesses to reach customers and for individuals to access goods and services in new and innovative ways."

Kato then turns his attention to the challenges posed by platform economics. "While platform economics offer tremendous opportunities for innovation and growth, they also present unique challenges, such as market concentration, data privacy, and regulatory concerns. It is essential that we address these challenges proactively to ensure that the benefits of platform economics are shared equitably and that consumers are protected."

A concerned citizen named Mumba raises her hand. "But how do we ensure that platform economics benefit not just a few large companies, but also smaller businesses and entrepreneurs? Are there strategies for promoting competition and innovation in platform ecosystems?"

Kato's expression brightens with determination. "Ah,

Mumba, an important question. Promoting competition and innovation in platform ecosystems requires a combination of regulatory oversight, market incentives, and technological innovation. This includes measures to prevent anti-competitive behavior, promote data portability and interoperability, and support the development of open standards and protocols."

He shares stories of successful initiatives from around the world that have promoted competition and innovation in platform ecosystems, from antitrust enforcement actions to open-source software projects. "By understanding and addressing the challenges of platform economics," Kato says, nodding to the crowd, "we can create a future where digital platforms are not only innovative and efficient but also fair and inclusive."

The audience nods in agreement, their faces reflecting a sense of determination and possibility.

Kato concludes with a call to action. "Let us embrace the opportunities presented by platform economics as we continue our journey towards economic prosperity and social inclusion. By harnessing the power of networks to drive innovation and create opportunities for all, we can build a future that is brighter and more inclusive for everyone in Ndola."

As the session draws to a close, the crowd disperses into the afternoon sunlight, their minds buzzing with excitement and possibility. With platform economics and network effects as their guide and community as their support, they are ready to embrace the opportunities of the digital age and shape a future that is both prosperous and equitable.

Sharing Economy and Collaborative Consumption

"Together We Thrive: Exploring the Sharing Economy and Collaborative Consumption"

As the day progresses in Ndola, the community center remains a hub of activity. Today's discussion on emerging trends in economics turns its focus to the sharing economy and collaborative consumption—a topic that promises to illuminate the power of community and cooperation in driving economic innovation.

Kato stands at the center of the room, his voice resonating with warmth and enthusiasm. "Good afternoon, everyone. Today, we embark on a journey into the world of the sharing economy and collaborative consumption—a realm where sharing is not just a virtue but a powerful economic force. Our goal is to explore how these principles are reshaping industries and communities, and how we can leverage them to build a more sustainable and equitable future."

He begins with a reflective tone. "The sharing economy is based on the idea of utilizing underutilized resources—whether they be physical assets, skills, or time—to create value for individuals and communities. It encompasses a wide range of activities, from peer-to-peer lending and ride-sharing to co-working spaces and community gardens. In Ndola, we are witnessing the emergence of sharing economy initiatives that are transforming the way we live, work, and interact."

The crowd listens intently, their eyes alight with curiosity and interest.

"Collaborative consumption," Kato explains, "takes the concept of sharing a step further by emphasizing the collective ownership and use of goods and services. It encourages individuals to share resources, reduce waste, and minimize environmental impact. In Ndola, collaborative consumption initiatives are empowering communities to come together to address shared challenges and create shared opportunities."

He gestures to a group of neighbors gathered in the corner, their hands busy at work as they share tools and expertise to build a community garden. "In Ndola, the sharing economy and collaborative consumption are fostering a culture of cooperation and resourcefulness, enabling individuals and communities to pool their resources and talents to create shared value."

Kato then turns his attention to the challenges and opportunities presented by these trends. "While the sharing economy and collaborative consumption offer tremendous benefits, they also present unique challenges, such as regulatory uncertainty, trust issues, and scalability concerns. It is essential that we address these challenges proactively to ensure that the benefits of these trends are shared equitably and that communities are empowered to participate fully in the sharing economy."

A concerned citizen named Mwape raises her hand. "But how do we ensure that the benefits of the sharing economy and collaborative consumption are accessible to all members of the community, especially those who may not have access to digital technologies or financial resources? Are there strategies for promoting inclusivity and accessibility in these initiatives?"

Kato's expression brightens with determination. "Ah, Mwape, an important question. Promoting inclusivity and accessibility in the sharing economy and collaborative consumption requires a multi-faceted approach that addresses barriers to participation, such as digital literacy, affordability, and cultural norms. This includes providing training and support to help individuals navigate the sharing economy, creating inclusive platforms and spaces that are accessible to all members of the community, and fostering a culture of trust and reciprocity."

He shares stories of successful initiatives from around the world that have promoted inclusivity and accessibility in the sharing economy and collaborative consumption, from community-led skill-sharing programs to government-sponsored initiatives to provide access to digital technologies and financial services. "By understanding and addressing the barriers to participation," Kato says, nodding to the crowd, "we can create a future where the benefits of the sharing economy and collaborative consumption are accessible to all members of the community, empowering individuals and communities to thrive together."

The audience nods in agreement, their faces reflecting a sense of determination and possibility.

Kato concludes with a call to action. "Let us embrace the opportunities presented by the sharing economy and collaborative consumption as we continue our journey towards economic prosperity and social inclusion. By harnessing the power of sharing and cooperation, we can build a future that is not only more sustainable and equitable but also more resilient and vibrant for everyone in Ndola."

As the session draws to a close, the crowd disperses into the afternoon sunlight, their hearts and minds filled with excitement and possibility. With the principles of the sharing economy and collaborative consumption as their guide and community as their support, they are ready to embrace the opportunities of collaboration and cooperation and shape a future that is both prosperous and inclusive.

Blockchain Technology and Cryptocurrencies

"Unraveling the Blockchain: Exploring the Promise of Blockchain Technology and Cryptocurrencies"

As the sun begins its descent over Ndola, the community center remains abuzz with energy. Today's discussion on emerging trends in economics delves into the world of blockchain technology and cryptocurrencies—an intriguing topic that promises to revolutionize traditional financial systems and unlock new opportunities for economic empowerment.

Kato stands before the eager crowd, his voice carrying a sense of anticipation and curiosity. "Good evening, everyone. Today, we embark on a journey into the realm of blockchain technology and cryptocurrencies—a world where innovation and decentralization converge to redefine the way we think about money, transactions, and trust. Our goal is to explore the potential of these technologies to reshape economic landscapes and empower individuals and communities."

He begins with a reflective tone. "Blockchain technology is a decentralized digital ledger that records transactions across a network of computers in a secure and transparent manner. By eliminating the need for intermediaries and providing immutable records of transactions, blockchain has the potential to revolutionize industries ranging from finance and supply chain management to healthcare and

CHAPTER 14: EMERGING TRENDS IN ECONOMICS

voting systems."

The crowd listens intently, their eyes alight with curiosity and intrigue.

"Cryptocurrencies," Kato explains, "are digital or virtual currencies that utilize blockchain technology to enable secure and decentralized transactions. Unlike traditional fiat currencies, which are issued and regulated by governments, cryptocurrencies operate independently of central authorities, allowing for greater autonomy and privacy in financial transactions."

He gestures to a group of young entrepreneurs gathered in the corner, their heads bent together in animated discussion as they discuss the potential applications of blockchain technology for their startup. "In Ndola, blockchain technology and cryptocurrencies are sparking a wave of innovation and entrepreneurship, empowering individuals to explore new ways of conducting business and accessing financial services."

Kato then turns his attention to the challenges and opportunities presented by these technologies. "While blockchain technology and cryptocurrencies offer tremendous promise, they also present unique challenges, such as scalability, regulatory uncertainty, and security concerns. It is essential that we address these challenges proactively to ensure that the benefits of these technologies are shared equitably and that communities are protected from potential risks."

A concerned citizen named Musa raises his hand. "But how do we ensure that blockchain technology and cryptocurrencies are accessible to all members of the community, especially those who may not have access to digital technologies or financial resources? Are there strategies for promoting inclusivity and accessibility in these technologies?"

Kato's expression brightens with determination. "Ah, Musa, an important question. Promoting inclusivity and accessibility in blockchain technology and cryptocurrencies requires a multi-faceted approach that addresses barriers to participation, such as digital literacy, affordability, and infrastructure. This includes providing education and training to help individuals understand and navigate blockchain technology, promoting the development of user-friendly interfaces and tools, and fostering partnerships with local organizations and governments to expand access to digital technologies and financial services."

He shares stories of successful initiatives from around the world that have promoted inclusivity and accessibility in blockchain technology and cryptocurrencies, from community-led blockchain education programs to government-sponsored initiatives to provide access to digital infrastructure and financial services. "By understanding and addressing the barriers to participation," Kato says, nodding to the crowd, "we can create a future where blockchain technology and cryptocurrencies empower individuals and communities to take control of their financial destinies, driving economic growth and prosperity for all."

The audience nods in agreement, their faces reflecting a sense of determination and possibility.

Kato concludes with a call to action. "Let us embrace the opportunities presented by blockchain technology and cryptocurrencies as we continue our journey towards economic prosperity and social inclusion. By harnessing the power of decentralization and innovation, we can build a future that is not only more resilient and transparent but also more equitable and inclusive for everyone in Ndola."

As the session draws to a close, the crowd disperses into the evening light, their hearts and minds filled with excitement and possibility. With blockchain technology and cryptocurrencies as their guide and community as their support, they are ready to embrace the opportunities of the digital age and shape a future that is both prosperous and inclusive.

Artificial Intelligence and Machine Learning in Economics

"The Intelligence of Tomorrow: Embracing Artificial Intelligence and Machine Learning in Economics"

As dusk settles over Ndola, the community center continues to pulse with energy. Today's discussion on emerging trends in economics delves into the transformative power of artificial intelligence (AI) and machine learning—an exciting topic that promises to revolutionize decision-making processes and unlock new pathways to economic growth and prosperity.

Kato stands amidst the gathering crowd, his voice resonating with a blend of excitement and curiosity. "Good evening, everyone. Today, we embark on a journey into the realm of artificial intelligence and machine learning—a world where algorithms and data converge to unlock new insights and possibilities. Our goal is to explore how these technologies are reshaping economic paradigms and empowering individuals and communities to navigate an ever-evolving landscape."

He begins with a reflective tone. "Artificial intelligence and machine learning refer to the use of computer algorithms to analyze data, identify patterns, and make predictions without explicit programming. These technologies have the potential to revolutionize economic analysis, decision-making processes, and policy formulation by providing policymakers, businesses, and individuals with powerful tools for understanding and navigating complex systems."

The crowd listens intently, their eyes alight with anticipation and curiosity.

"Artificial intelligence," Kato explains, "encompasses a wide range of techniques and applications, from predictive analytics and natural language processing to autonomous systems and robotics. In Ndola, we are witnessing the impact of artificial intelligence and machine learning across various sectors, from healthcare and agriculture to transportation and finance, creating new opportunities for innovation and growth."

He gestures to a group of young entrepreneurs gathered in the corner, their heads bent together in animated discussion as they discuss the potential applications of AI and machine learning for their startup. "In Ndola, artificial intelligence and machine learning are driving entrepreneurship and creativity, empowering individuals to develop solutions to pressing challenges and unlock new pathways to economic prosperity."

Kato then turns his attention to the challenges and opportunities presented by these technologies. "While artificial intelligence and machine learning offer tremendous promise, they also present unique challenges, such as data privacy, algorithmic bias, and ethical concerns. It is essential that we address these challenges proactively to ensure that the benefits of these technologies are shared equitably and that communities are protected from potential risks."

A concerned citizen named Temwani raises her hand. "But how do we ensure that artificial intelligence and machine learning are used responsibly and ethically, especially in sensitive areas such as healthcare and finance? Are there strategies for promoting transparency and accountability in the development and deployment of these technologies?"

Kato's expression brightens with determination. "Ah, Temwani, an important question. Promoting transparency and accountability in artificial intelligence and machine learning requires a multi-faceted approach that involves stakeholders from across society, including policymakers, researchers, industry leaders, and civil society organizations. This includes developing ethical guidelines and best practices for the development and deployment of AI systems, promoting transparency and explainability in algorithmic decision-making processes, and fostering partnerships between government, industry, and academia to address emerging challenges and opportunities."

He shares stories of successful initiatives from around the world that have promoted transparency and accountability in artificial intelligence and machine learning, from open-source AI projects to multi-stakeholder collaborations on AI ethics and governance. "By understanding and addressing the ethical and social implications of AI," Kato says, nodding to the crowd, "we can create a future where artificial intelligence and machine learning empower individuals and communities to make informed decisions and build a more equitable and inclusive society."

The audience nods in agreement, their faces reflecting a sense of determination and possibility.

Kato concludes with a call to action. "Let us embrace the opportunities presented by artificial intelligence and machine learning as we continue our journey towards economic prosperity and social inclusion. By harnessing the power of data and algorithms to drive innovation and empower individuals, we can build a future that is not only more intelligent and efficient but also more ethical and compassionate for everyone in Ndola."

As the session draws to a close, the crowd disperses into the night, their hearts and minds filled with excitement and possibility. With artificial intelligence and machine learning as their guide and community as their support, they are ready to embrace the opportunities of the digital age and shape a future that is both prosperous and just.

Implications of Automation for Labor Markets

"Navigating the Automation Era: Understanding the Implications for Labor Markets"

As night falls over Ndola, the community center remains illuminated, buzzing with anticipation for the next segment of the discussion on emerging trends in economics. Tonight's focus turns to the profound implications of automation for labor markets—an urgent topic that promises to reshape the future of work and economic opportunity.

Kato stands before the attentive crowd, his voice projecting a mix of concern and determination. "Good evening, everyone. Tonight, we embark on a crucial exploration into the implications of automation for labor markets—a journey that will shed light on the challenges and opportunities presented by the rise of technology in the workplace. Our goal is to understand how automation is reshaping industries, transforming job roles, and shaping the future of economic opportunity for individuals and communities."

He begins with a solemn tone. "Automation refers to the use of technology, such as robotics, artificial intelligence, and machine learning, to perform tasks traditionally carried out by humans. While automation has the potential to increase productivity, improve efficiency, and drive innovation, it also poses significant challenges for labor markets, including job displacement, wage stagnation, and skills mismatches."

The crowd listens intently, their expressions reflecting a mix of apprehension and curiosity.

"In Ndola," Kato explains, "we are witnessing the impact of automation across various sectors, from manufacturing and transportation to retail and customer service. As robots and algorithms increasingly take on routine and repetitive tasks, many workers find themselves facing uncertainty about the future of their jobs and livelihoods."

He gestures to a group of concerned workers gathered in the corner, their voices hushed as they discuss the potential impact of automation on their industries. "In Ndola, the implications of automation for labor markets are palpable, prompting workers and policymakers alike to grapple with the challenges of adapting to a rapidly changing economic landscape."

Kato then turns his attention to the opportunities presented by automation. "While automation poses challenges for labor markets, it also presents opportunities for innovation, creativity, and economic growth. By freeing workers from routine tasks, automation has the potential to empower individuals to focus on higher-value activities, such as problem-solving, critical thinking, and creativity."

A concerned citizen named Chola raises his hand. "But

how do we ensure that the benefits of automation are shared equitably among workers, especially those in vulnerable industries and communities? Are there strategies for promoting reskilling and upskilling to prepare workers for the jobs of the future?"

Kato's expression brightens with determination. "Ah, Chola, an important question. Promoting equitable access to the benefits of automation requires a multi-faceted approach that addresses the needs of workers, businesses, and communities. This includes investing in education and training programs to equip workers with the skills they need to thrive in a digital economy, supporting entrepreneurship and innovation to create new opportunities for economic growth, and implementing policies that promote fair wages, worker protections, and social safety nets."

He shares stories of successful initiatives from around the world that have promoted reskilling and upskilling, from government-sponsored training programs to industry-led partnerships with educational institutions. "By understanding and addressing the challenges of automation," Kato says, nodding to the crowd, "we can create a future where technology empowers individuals and communities to thrive in a rapidly changing world."

The audience nods in agreement, their faces reflecting a mix of concern and determination.

Kato concludes with a call to action. "Let us embrace the opportunities presented by automation as we continue our journey towards economic prosperity and social inclusion. By harnessing the power of technology to drive innovation, empower workers, and build stronger, more resilient communities, we can shape a future that is not only more efficient and productive but also more equitable and just for everyone in Ndola."

As the session draws to a close, the crowd disperses into the night, their hearts and minds filled with a renewed sense of purpose and possibility. With automation as their guide and community as their support, they are ready to embrace the challenges and opportunities of the automation era and shape a future that is both prosperous and humane.

15

Chapter 15: Economics and Society

Economic Sociology and Social Embeddedness

"Weaving the Fabric of Society: Exploring Economic Sociology and Social Embeddedness"

In the heart of Ndola, the community center hums with anticipation for the final segment of the discussion on emerging trends in economics. Tonight's focus turns to the intricate relationship between economics and society—a captivating topic that delves into the social dynamics shaping economic behavior and outcomes.

Kato steps forward, his presence commanding attention amidst the eager crowd. "Good evening, everyone. Tonight, we embark on a profound exploration into the intersection of economics and society—a journey that will illuminate the interconnectedness of human relationships, institutions, and culture in shaping economic processes and outcomes. Our goal is to understand how economic sociology and the concept of social embeddedness offer invaluable insights into the complex fabric of our social and economic lives."

He begins with a contemplative tone. "Economic sociology is a branch of sociology that examines the social and cultural factors influencing economic behavior, institutions, and outcomes. At its core is the concept of social embeddedness, which emphasizes the idea that economic activities are deeply intertwined with social relations, norms, and structures."

The crowd listens intently, their curiosity piqued by the promise of unraveling the intricate web of societal influences on economics.

"In Ndola," Kato explains, "we can see the principles of economic sociology and social embeddedness at work in various aspects of our daily lives. From informal markets and community savings groups to traditional kinship networks and religious organizations, social relationships and networks play a central role in shaping economic transactions, resource allocation, and wealth distribution."

He gestures to a group of community leaders gathered in the corner, their heads bent together in earnest discussion as they strategize ways to support local entrepreneurs and promote economic development. "In Ndola, economic sociology and social embeddedness are evident in the close-knit fabric of our communities, where trust, reciprocity, and shared norms serve as the foundation for economic activities and social cohesion."

Kato then turns his attention to the implications of economic sociology for understanding and addressing societal challenges. "By recognizing the social embeddedness of economic activities, we gain a deeper understanding of the root causes of economic inequality, poverty, and social exclusion. This allows us to develop more holistic and effective strategies for promoting economic development, social inclusion, and community resilience."

A concerned citizen named Ngozi raises her hand. "But how do we leverage the principles of economic sociology and social embeddedness to address pressing challenges such as poverty and inequality in our community? Are there strategies for fostering social cohesion and solidarity to support economic development and wellbeing?"

Kato's expression brightens with optimism. "Ah, Ngozi, an important question. Leveraging the principles of economic sociology and social embeddedness requires a multi-faceted approach that involves collaboration and partnership between individuals, communities, governments, and organizations. This includes promoting inclusive economic policies and programs that prioritize the needs of marginalized groups, strengthening social safety nets and support networks to provide assistance and opportunities for those in need, and fostering a culture of solidarity and reciprocity that values the wellbeing of all members of society."

He shares stories of successful initiatives from around the world that have leveraged the principles of economic sociology and social embeddedness to promote economic development and social cohesion, from community-led development projects to government-sponsored programs that prioritize social equity and inclusion. "By embracing the principles of economic sociology," Kato says, nodding to the crowd, "we can build a future where economic prosperity is not only sustainable and inclusive but also deeply rooted in the bonds of community and solidarity."

The audience nods in agreement, their faces reflecting a mix of contemplation and determination.

Kato concludes with a call to action. "Let us embrace the principles of economic sociology and social embeddedness as we continue our journey towards economic prosperity and social justice. By recognizing the interconnectedness of our economic and social lives, and by working together to build stronger, more resilient communities, we can shape a future that is not only more prosperous and equitable but also more compassionate and humane for everyone in Ndola."

As the session draws to a close, the crowd disperses into the night, their hearts and minds filled with a renewed sense of purpose and solidarity. With economic sociology as their guide and community as their support, they are ready to embark on the journey of shaping a future that honors the richness and complexity of human relationships and fosters shared prosperity for all.

Inequality and Social Mobility

"Bridging the Divide: Navigating Inequality and Fostering Social Mobility"

In the heart of Ndola, amidst the vibrant energy of the community center, the discussion on economics and society continues to unfold. Tonight's focus shifts towards the intricate dynamics of inequality and the quest for social mobility—an imperative exploration into the barriers and opportunities that shape the economic landscape of the city.

Kato takes center stage once more, his voice resonating with a blend of empathy and determination. "Good evening, everyone. Tonight, we embark on a profound journey into the heart of inequality and social mobility—a journey that will illuminate the stark realities of economic disparity and the pathways towards a more equitable future. Our goal is to understand how inequality impacts our communities and how fostering social mobility can pave the way towards greater economic opportunity for all."

He begins with a sobering tone. "Inequality, both in income and opportunity, is a pressing issue that affects communities worldwide, and Ndola is no exception. From disparities in access to education and healthcare to unequal distribution of wealth and resources, the effects of inequality are deeply felt across our city, shaping the life chances and prospects of individuals and families."

The crowd listens intently, their faces reflecting a mix of concern and resolve.

"In Ndola," Kato continues, "inequality manifests itself in various forms, from disparities in income and wealth to differences in access to quality education and employment opportunities. These inequalities not only perpetuate social divisions but also hinder economic growth and undermine the fabric of our society."

He gestures to a group of young students gathered in the corner, their expressions determined as they discuss strategies for overcoming the barriers to higher education. "In Ndola, the quest for social mobility is a driving force for many individuals and families, as they strive to overcome the obstacles of poverty and inequality to create a better future for themselves and their communities."

Kato then turns his attention to the pathways towards fostering social mobility. "By addressing the root causes of inequality and investing in strategies that promote social mobility, we can create a more inclusive and equitable society where everyone has the opportunity to thrive and succeed. This includes expanding access to quality education and healthcare, investing in job training and skills development programs, and implementing policies that promote fair wages, affordable housing, and social safety nets."

A concerned citizen named Mutale raises her hand. "But how do we break the cycle of intergenerational poverty and inequality in our community? Are there strategies for creating more equitable systems and structures that support upward mobility for all?"

Kato's expression softens with empathy. "Ah, Mutale, an important question. Breaking the cycle of intergenerational poverty and inequality requires a concerted effort from all sectors of society. This includes addressing systemic barriers to opportunity, such as discrimination, lack of access to resources, and unequal distribution of power and privilege. It also requires fostering a culture of inclusion and solidarity that values the dignity and worth of every individual."

He shares stories of successful initiatives from around the world that have promoted social mobility and reduced inequality, from targeted interventions to support disadvantaged youth to policies that promote fair taxation and wealth redistribution. "By working together," Kato says, nodding to the crowd, "we can create a future where everyone has the opportunity to fulfill their potential and contribute to the prosperity of our community."

The audience nods in agreement, their faces reflecting a mix of determination and hope.

Kato concludes with a call to action. "Let us embrace the challenge of inequality and social mobility as we continue our journey towards a more just and equitable society. By recognizing the inherent worth and potential of every individual, and by working together to create systems and structures that support upward mobility for all, we can build a future where opportunity knows no bounds and prosperity is shared by all in Ndola."

As the session draws to a close, the crowd disperses into the night, their hearts and minds filled with a renewed sense of purpose and solidarity. With inequality and social mobility as their guide and community as their support, they are ready to embark on the journey of building a future where everyone has the opportunity to thrive and succeed.

Poverty Alleviation Strategies

"Rising Together: Unveiling Strategies for Poverty Alleviation"

In the heart of Ndola, under the warm glow of the community center's lights, the conversation on economics and society unfolds further. Tonight's focus turns towards the urgent task of poverty alleviation—an exploration into the strategies and initiatives that hold the promise of uplifting the most vulnerable members of the community.

Kato stands before the assembled crowd once more, his voice filled with compassion and resolve. "Good evening, everyone. Tonight, we embark on a vital exploration into the realm of poverty alleviation—a journey that will shed light on the challenges of economic hardship and the pathways towards a brighter future for all. Our goal is to uncover the strategies and initiatives that can empower individuals and communities to break free from the cycle of poverty and build a more prosperous and inclusive society."

He begins with a solemn acknowledgment. "Poverty is a harsh reality for far too many in Ndola, depriving individuals and families of their dignity, their opportunities, and their dreams for the future. It is a complex and multifaceted issue, rooted in systemic inequalities, social exclusion, and economic injustice."

The crowd listens intently, their faces reflecting a mix of empathy and determination.

"In Ndola," Kato continues, "poverty manifests itself in various forms, from inadequate access to basic necessities such as food, shelter, and healthcare to limited opportunities for education, employment, and economic mobility. These challenges not only perpetuate suffering and hardship but also hinder the overall development and prosperity of our community."

He gestures to a group of community leaders gathered in the corner, their heads bowed in deep discussion as they strategize ways to support vulnerable families and individuals. "In Ndola, the fight against poverty is a collective endeavor, as individuals and organizations come together to provide assistance, resources, and hope to those in need."

Kato then turns his attention to the strategies for poverty alleviation. "By addressing the root causes of poverty and implementing targeted interventions, we can create pathways towards a more equitable and inclusive society where everyone has the opportunity to thrive and succeed. This includes expanding access to education and healthcare, promoting sustainable livelihoods and economic opportunities, and strengthening social safety nets and support networks for the most vulnerable members of our community."

A concerned citizen named Mwansa raises her hand. "But how do we ensure that our efforts to alleviate poverty are effective and sustainable in the long term? Are there strategies for promoting empowerment and resilience among those living in poverty?"

Kato's expression softens with empathy. "Ah, Mwansa, an important question. Ensuring the effectiveness and sustainability of poverty alleviation efforts requires a holistic and multi-faceted approach that addresses the complex and interconnected factors contributing to poverty. This includes empowering individuals and communities to take ownership of their own development, fostering partnerships and collaboration between government, civil society, and the private sector, and promoting policies and programs that prioritize the needs and aspirations of those living in poverty."

He shares stories of successful poverty alleviation initiatives from around the world, from microfinance programs that empower women entrepreneurs to community-led development projects that promote sustainable livelihoods and economic resilience. "By working together," Kato says, nodding to the crowd, "we can create a future where poverty is not only alleviated but where every individual has the opportunity to live with dignity, security, and hope."

The audience nods in agreement, their faces reflecting a mix of determination and hope.

Kato concludes with a call to action. "Let us embrace the challenge of poverty alleviation as we continue our journey towards a more just and compassionate society. By recognizing the inherent worth and potential of every individual, and by working together to create systems and structures that support empowerment, resilience, and opportunity for all, we can build a future where poverty is but a distant memory, and prosperity is shared by all in Ndola."

As the session draws to a close, the crowd disperses into the night, their hearts and minds filled with a renewed sense of purpose and solidarity. With poverty alleviation as their guide and community as their support, they are ready to embark on the journey of building a future where no one is left behind, and where everyone has the opportunity to thrive and flourish.

Poverty Alleviation Strategies

"Empowering Dreams: Unveiling Strategies for Poverty Alleviation"

In the heart of Ndola, within the embrace of the community center, the conversation on economics and society continues to unfold. Tonight, the spotlight shines on the urgent task of poverty alleviation—a journey into the transformative strategies that promise to uplift the most vulnerable members of society.

Kato steps forward, his presence a beacon of hope amidst the attentive crowd. "Good evening, everyone. Tonight, we embark on a vital exploration into the realm of poverty alleviation—a journey that will illuminate the pathways towards dignity, opportunity, and a brighter future for all. Our goal is to unveil the strategies and initiatives that can break the chains of poverty and cultivate a landscape of prosperity and inclusivity."

He begins with a somber acknowledgment. "Poverty casts a long shadow over Ndola, robbing individuals of their aspirations, their potential, and their basic needs. It is a silent oppressor, perpetuating cycles of deprivation and despair that echo through generations."

The crowd listens intently, their eyes reflecting a mix of empathy and resolve.

"In Ndola," Kato continues, "poverty is a harsh reality for too many, manifested in hunger, inadequate housing, and limited access to education and healthcare. Yet, amidst the darkness, there are sparks of hope—individuals and organizations committed to rewriting the narrative of despair into one of empowerment and opportunity."

He gestures to a group of volunteers huddled in discussion, their faces alight with determination as they plan the next phase of their community-driven initiative. "In Ndola, the fight against poverty is not a solitary endeavor but a collective mission, fueled by compassion, collaboration, and unwavering determination."

Kato then turns his attention to the strategies for poverty alleviation. "By addressing the root causes of poverty and harnessing the power of innovation and collaboration, we can pave the way towards a more equitable and prosperous society. This includes empowering communities through access to education and skills training, fostering entrepreneurship and economic development, and implementing social safety nets that provide a lifeline for those in need."

A voice rises from the crowd, filled with concern and determination. "But how do we ensure that our efforts yield lasting impact, that they ignite flames of hope that endure beyond the present moment? Are there strategies for nurturing resilience and self-reliance among those battling the chains of poverty?"

Kato's expression softens with empathy. "Ah, my friend, an important question indeed. Ensuring the sustainability and resilience of our efforts demands a holistic approach—one that fosters empowerment, resilience, and self-reliance among individuals and communities. It requires a commitment to nurturing not only economic opportunities but also the human spirit—the resilience, ingenuity, and dignity that reside within each and every one of us."

He shares stories of hope and transformation, of individuals who, against all odds, dared to dream and toil for a better tomorrow. "By investing in the potential and agency of every individual, by fostering partnerships and collaboration, and by championing policies and programs that prioritize dignity and opportunity, we can build a future where poverty is not a life sentence but a chapter in a story of resilience and triumph."

The audience nods in agreement, their hearts stirred by the promise of a brighter tomorrow.

Kato concludes with a call to action. "Let us embrace the challenge of poverty alleviation as a shared mission—a journey towards a future where every individual has the opportunity to thrive, to flourish, and to realize their full potential. Together, let us weave a tapestry of dignity, opportunity, and hope—a tapestry that spans generations and transcends barriers, illuminating the path towards a more just and compassionate Ndola."

As the session draws to a close, the crowd disperses into the night, their hearts ablaze with the promise of a future where dreams know no bounds, and where every voice, every dream, and every life is cherished and empowered to soar.

Corporate Social Responsibility and Business Ethics

"Ethical Horizons: Navigating Corporate Social Responsibility and Business Ethics"

In the heart of Ndola, amidst the hushed whispers of the community center, the discussion on economics and society takes a poignant turn. Tonight, the spotlight shines on the ethical compass of businesses and the transformative power of corporate social responsibility—a journey into the heart of values and impact.

Kato strides purposefully to the center stage, his gaze steady, his voice a clarion call for conscience amidst the crowd. "Good evening, esteemed guests. Tonight, we embark on a vital exploration into the realm of corporate social responsibility and business ethics—a journey that illuminates the profound impact of values-driven businesses in shaping the fabric of our society. Our quest is to unravel the threads of conscience and compassion that bind together the worlds of commerce and community."

He begins with a solemn acknowledgment. "In the marketplace of Ndola, businesses wield immense power—not only to generate wealth but also to catalyze social change and uplift the lives of the marginalized. Yet, with this power comes a profound responsibility—a responsibility to conduct business with integrity, empathy, and a steadfast commitment to the common good."

The crowd listens intently, their eyes alight with a mix of curiosity and expectation.

"In Ndola," Kato continues, "the principles of corporate social responsibility and business ethics find resonance in the actions of businesses large and small, from neighborhood enterprises to multinational corporations. These businesses understand that their success is intertwined with the wellbeing of the communities they serve and the environment they inhabit."

He gestures to a group of entrepreneurs gathered in earnest discussion, their voices animated as they debate ways to integrate sustainability practices into their operations. "In Ndola, the pursuit of profit is not divorced from the pursuit of purpose. It is a harmonious convergence—a recognition that business success is measured not only in monetary gains but also in the positive impact it creates for people and planet."

Kato then turns his attention to the essence of corporate social responsibility. "By embracing principles of ethical conduct, environmental stewardship, and social accountability, businesses can become powerful agents of change—catalysts for progress, inclusivity, and sustainability. This includes investing in initiatives that benefit local communities, reducing environmental footprint, promoting diversity and inclusion in the workplace, and upholding transparent and ethical business practices."

A voice rises from the audience, filled with curiosity and concern. "But how do we ensure that businesses uphold these lofty ideals and do not succumb to the temptations of profit at any cost? Are there mechanisms in place to hold them accountable for their actions and ensure they walk the path of integrity and social responsibility?"

Kato's expression softens with empathy. "Ah, my friend, a question of paramount importance. Ensuring businesses uphold their ethical obligations demands not only vigilance but also collaboration between stakeholders—governments, civil society, consumers, and employees. It requires the establishment of robust regulatory frameworks, transparent reporting mechanisms, and a culture of accountability that leaves no room for compromise."

He shares stories of businesses that have embraced the principles of corporate social responsibility, from initiatives to combat climate change to programs that promote fair labor practices and community development. "By championing a values-driven approach to business, by holding themselves accountable to their stakeholders, and by fostering a culture of ethics and integrity, businesses can become beacons of positive change in our society."

The audience nods in agreement, their hearts stirred by the promise of a new paradigm of business—one rooted in conscience and compassion.

Kato concludes with a call to action. "Let us embrace the ideals of corporate social responsibility and business ethics as guiding stars on our journey towards a more just and sustainable future. Together, let us forge a path of integrity, empathy, and responsibility—a path that leads to prosperity not only for businesses but for all in Ndola and beyond."

As the session draws to a close, the crowd disperses into the night, their minds ignited with the possibilities of a business world guided by conscience and compassion. With corporate social responsibility as their compass and community as their compass, they are ready to chart a new course towards a future where business thrives, and humanity flourishes in harmony with the world around them.

Economic Rights and Social Justice

"Harmony of Rights: Advocating for Economic Justice and Social Equity"

Within the heart of Ndola, amid the communal embrace of the community center, the discourse on economics and society takes a poignant turn. Tonight, the stage is set to illuminate the profound intersection of economic rights and social justice—a journey into the fabric of equality and empowerment.

Kato strides forward, his presence commanding the attention of the gathered audience. "Good evening, esteemed guests. Tonight, we embark on a journey of advocacy and empowerment—an exploration into the inherent rights of every individual to economic dignity and social equity. Our quest is to illuminate the path towards a society where justice is not a privilege but a fundamental cornerstone of our collective humanity."

He begins with a solemn acknowledgment. "In the tapestry of Ndola's community, economic rights and social justice are the threads that bind us together—uniting us in our quest for dignity, equality, and opportunity. Yet, for too many among us, these rights remain elusive, obscured by the shadows of inequality and injustice."

The audience listens intently, their faces a reflection of empathy and determination.

"In Ndola," Kato continues, "the pursuit of economic rights and social justice is a clarion call—a call to dismantle the barriers that divide us and to build a society where every individual, regardless of background or circumstance, can realize their full potential and contribute to the common good."

He gestures to a group of activists gathered in spirited conversation, their voices rising in solidarity as they discuss strategies for advancing economic rights and social justice. "In Ndola, the fight for justice is not waged in isolation but in unity—with communities coming together to demand accountability, transparency, and equity from those in positions of power."

Kato then turns his attention to the essence of economic rights and social justice. "By championing the rights of the marginalized, by advocating for policies and programs that promote economic empowerment and social inclusion, we can create a society where every individual has the opportunity to thrive and flourish. This includes ensuring access to quality education, healthcare, and housing, promoting fair wages and dignified work, and upholding the principles of equality and non-discrimination in all aspects of life."

A voice rises from the audience, filled with passion and conviction. "But how do we ensure that the voices of the marginalized are heard, that their rights are respected, and their dignity upheld? Are there mechanisms in place to hold institutions and policymakers accountable for advancing economic justice and social equity?"

Kato's expression softens with empathy. "Ah, my friend, a question that strikes at the heart of our collective struggle. Ensuring economic rights and social justice demands not only vigilance but also advocacy—advocacy for policies and practices that prioritize the needs and aspirations of the most vulnerable among us. It requires amplifying the voices of the marginalized, empowering communities to demand change, and holding institutions accountable for their actions."

He shares stories of communities that have mobilized for change, from grassroots movements to legal battles for justice and equality. "By standing in solidarity with one another, by advocating for policies and practices that prioritize economic rights and social justice, and by fostering a culture of empathy, compassion, and inclusion, we can build a future where justice is not an aspiration but a reality for all in Ndola and beyond."

The audience nods in agreement, their hearts stirred by the promise of a more just and equitable society.

Kato concludes with a call to action. "Let us embrace the cause of economic rights and social justice as a collective imperative—a journey towards a future where every individual is treated with dignity, respect, and compassion. Together, let us weave a tapestry of justice, equality, and empowerment—a tapestry that spans generations, transcends boundaries, and illuminates the path towards a more just and compassionate Ndola."

As the session draws to a close, the crowd disperses into the night, their minds ablaze with the promise of a future where justice reigns supreme, and every individual has the opportunity to flourish and thrive. With economic rights as their guiding star and social justice as their compass, they are ready to embark on the journey of building a society where every voice is heard, every right respected, and every dream realized.

Economics as a Tool for Social Change

"Transformative Visions: Harnessing Economics for Social Change"

Amidst the warmth of Ndola's community center, the discussion on economics and society takes a transformative turn. Tonight, the stage is set to explore the profound potential of economics as a catalyst for social change—a journey into the realm of innovation, empowerment, and collective action.

Kato steps forward, his presence a beacon of hope amidst the assembled audience. "Good evening, esteemed guests. Tonight, we embark on a journey of possibility—a journey into the transformative power of economics as a force for social change. Our quest is to illuminate the pathways towards a more just, equitable, and inclusive society, where every individual has the opportunity to thrive and contribute to the common good."

He begins with a solemn acknowledgment. "In the landscape of Ndola's community, economics is more than just numbers and transactions—it is a vehicle for progress, a tool for empowerment, and a force for social transformation. Yet, for too long, the promise of economics has been overshadowed by inequality, injustice, and exclusion."

The audience listens intently, their eyes alight with curiosity and determination.

"In Ndola," Kato continues, "the vision of economics as a force for social change is a rallying cry—a call to action for individuals, communities, and institutions to come together in pursuit of a brighter future. It is a vision that transcends boundaries, unites hearts, and empowers minds to dream, innovate, and create."

He gestures to a group of young activists gathered in spirited discussion, their voices rising in passion as they strategize ways to harness the tools of economics for social good. "In Ndola, the movement for social change is alive and thriving—with young people leading the charge, advocating for justice, equality, and opportunity for all."

Kato then turns his attention to the essence of economics as a tool for social change. "By reimagining the role of economics in our society, by centering values of justice, equity, and sustainability, we can unlock new possibilities for transformative change. This includes leveraging economic policies and programs to address systemic inequalities, investing in social infrastructure and human capital, and amplifying the voices of marginalized communities in decision-making processes."

A voice rises from the audience, filled with hope and conviction. "But how do we ensure that economics serves the interests of all, and not just a privileged few? Are there strategies for democratizing economic power and promoting inclusive growth?"

Kato's expression softens with empathy. "Ah, my friend, a question that lies at the heart of our collective endeavor. Ensuring that economics serves the interests of all demands not only bold action but also a commitment to participatory decision-making, equitable distribution of resources, and meaningful engagement with diverse stakeholders. It requires fostering a culture of transparency, accountability, and collaboration—a culture where everyone has a seat at the table and a voice in shaping the future."

He shares stories of communities that have embraced economics as a tool for social change, from grassroots initiatives to policy reforms that prioritize human wellbeing over profit margins. "By harnessing the power of economics for social good, by building bridges of understanding and solidarity, and by working together towards a common vision of justice and equity, we can create a future where every individual has the opportunity to thrive, to contribute, and to live with dignity and purpose."

The audience nods in agreement, their hearts stirred by the promise of a more just and equitable society.

Kato concludes with a call to action. "Let us embrace the vision of economics as a force for social change as a guiding principle on our journey towards a more just, equitable, and inclusive Ndola. Together, let us weave a tapestry of possibility, empowerment, and collective action—a tapestry that spans generations, transcends boundaries, and illuminates the path towards a brighter future for all."

As the session draws to a close, the crowd disperses into the night, their minds ignited with the promise of a future where economics serves as a catalyst for social change, and every individual has the opportunity to contribute to a more just and equitable world. With economics as their guide and solidarity as their strength, they are ready to embark on the journey of building a society where every dream is possible, and every life is valued and empowered to flourish.

About the Author

Goodson Mumba is a multifaceted individual known for his diverse expertise and prolific contributions across various fields. As an infopreneur, thought leader, and spiritual leader, he has inspired countless individuals through his insightful teachings and impactful writings. Mumba is also an accomplished author, with several notable works to his name, including "Understanding Corporate Worship," "The Years I Spent in a Week," "Management By Harmony," "The CEO's Diary," "Change to Change" and "Creative Thinking for results" His literary works span topics ranging from business management to personal development and spirituality, reflecting his broad range of interests and insights.

With a Master of Business Leadership (MBL) and a Bachelor of Arts in Theology (BTh), Mumba brings a unique blend of business acumen and spiritual wisdom to his work. His educational background is further enriched by a Group Diploma in Management Studies, providing him with a solid foundation in organizational dynamics and leadership principles. Additionally, Mumba holds diplomas in Education Psychology, Leadership and Management Styles, Organizational Behaviour, Financial Accounting, Economic Growth and Development, and Project Management, showcasing his commitment to continuous learning and professional development.

Mumba's expertise extends beyond traditional academic disciplines, encompassing areas such as Neuro-Linguistic Programming (NLP) and Positive Psychology. His diverse skill set is complemented by a range of certifications, including Creative Problem Solving and Decision Making, Life Coaching Fundamentals and Techniques, Professional Life Coaching, and Performance Management System Design. These certifications reflect Mumba's dedication to equipping himself with the tools and knowledge necessary to empower others and drive positive change.

As an author, Mumba's writings reflect his deep understanding of human nature, organizational dynamics, and spiritual principles. His works offer practical insights, actionable strategies, and inspirational guidance for individuals seeking personal growth, professional success, and spiritual fulfillment. Mumba's holistic approach to life and leadership resonates with readers worldwide, making him a respected figure in both the business and spiritual communities.

Overall, Goodson Mumba's diverse background, extensive knowledge, and profound insights make him a sought-after speaker, mentor, and author. His commitment to excellence, lifelong learning, and service to others continues to inspire individuals to unlock their full potential and lead lives of purpose and significance.

Goodson Mumba is renowned for initiating the concept of Management by Harmony, revolutionizing traditional management practices with a focus on balanced and holistic approaches. He has authored two influential books on this subject: "Introduction to Management by Harmony" and its sequel, "Management by Harmony."

Mumba's work has significantly impacted the field, offering innovative strategies for fostering organizational harmony and efficiency. His contributions continue to shape contemporary management theories and practices.

www.ingramcontent.com/pod-product-compliance
Lightning Source LLC
Chambersburg PA
CBHW071826210526
45479CB00001B/9